# ARTS EDUCATION

## beyond the classroom

Edited by Judith H. Balfe and Joni Cherbo Heine

ACA BOOKS
American Council for the Arts
New York New York

**ACA Arts Research Seminar Series Coordinator: Sarah Foote**

Edited by Barbara Ryan
Jacket design by Joel Weltman, Duffy & Weltman

Director of Publishing: Robert Porter
Assistant Director of Publishing: Amy Jennings

**Library of Congress Cataloging in Publication Data:**

Arts Education Beyond the Classroom.

(ACA arts research seminar series; 2) Bibliography: p.
1. Arts — Study and teaching — United States.   I. Balfe, Judith H.
II. Heine, Joni Cherbo.   III. Series
NX303.A73    1988          700'.7150973          88-22346
ISBN 0-915400-72-3 (pbk.)

*The ACA Arts Research Seminar Program
was made possible by a generous grant
from the Reed Foundation*

## ABOUT THE EDITORS

**Judith H. Balfe** is assistant professor of sociology at the College of Staten Island–City University of New York. Previously, she was lecturer in sociology at Rutgers University. She holds a Ph.D. from Rutgers University and has worked on educational programs at the Newark Museum and the Boston Museum of Fine Arts. She lectures and writes frequently on the arts in society.

**Joni Cherbo Heine** is a Ph.D. sociologist who specializes in the arts. She is presently on the faculty of New York University's graduate arts administration program and has been on the faculty of Lehman College and Columbia University Presbyterian Hospital, Behavioral Science Department. She has served as an education consultant at the International Center of Photography and has been an assistant in research projects in family and historical/comparative sociology. Her published work includes articles and papers on the sociology of art.

# CONTENTS

# ACKNOWLEDGMENTS

With this volume, ACA marks the publication of the second monograph in the ACA Arts Research Seminar series. Its content has been shaped and molded from the spirited presentation and discussion of ideas which took place at a March 1987 arts research seminar in New York City. Unlike other issues, arts education for adults—because it is a relatively new field—could not be considered against a history rich with analysis, facts and research. Instead, we relied upon the recounting of the personal experiences of a diverse, talented group of pioneers in the field. For whatever measure of success we are able to achieve in advancing the field with this publication, credit must go in large part to those who so unselfishly have shared their insight and knowledge on the succeeding pages. Thank you all.

No words can express our appreciation to Judy Balfe and Joni Heine, whose task it was to shape a subject which began as a notion about a field largely undefined. Their hours of tireless, dedicated effort in assembling the seminar and in editing this volume are evident by the result. I extend to them our deepest gratitude.

Finally, I would like to thank the Reed Foundation for their belief in the Arts Research Seminars program and for their continued support. May the sum of all these efforts contribute in some small way to securing a prosperous future for the arts in this country.

SARAH FOOTE
Coordinator
Arts Research Seminars

# introduction

# ON THE NECESSITY OF ADULT ARTS EDUCATION BEYOND THE CLASSROOM

## by Judith H. Balfe and Joni Cherbo Heine

Learning is a lifetime experience. It does not cease with the acquisition of a degree. Inevitably people continue to learn, whether in informal or in structured settings. To advocate arts education for adults, as the participants in this seminar are doing, is to reject the common view that programs of adult education are by definition not serious or too late to make any difference. The "lifelong learning" movement has worked to change both the educational philosophy and the developmental psychology that reinforced such limiting perspectives. It is time for arts educators to get aboard.

The extraordinary growth in the arts over the last 20 years is encouraging. Attendance at arts events now surpasses that at sports events; more people go to museums than to football games. In the 1985 Bureau of the Census survey of arts participation, 40 percent of all adults in the United States reported attendance at one or more arts events in the preceding year. The mass media appear to be stimulating arts participation rather than competing with it. The people who watch Luciano Pavarotti on television and listen to radio and recordings are far more likely to be part of the live opera audience than are those who do not.

However, there is evidence for some concern about the continued health of the arts. Although the arts have a growing hold on the U.S. public, more than 60 percent of adults do not participate in the arts at all, and many who do so are only marginally involved. If this gap is ignored, a serious erosion in the quantity and quality of arts participation in society may take place. The perpetuation of the arts is dependent upon enriching existing audiences and educating the widest population possible in the practice and history of art and aesthetics, so that all may participate more fully in the culture of our time.

Of those "beyond the classroom," foremost in numbers are the "baby boomers," now representing a full third of the total U.S. population and more than 60 percent of the electorate. Higher education generally remains the strongest predictor of arts participation, and baby boomers have received proportionately more higher education than those who are older. Yet they are seriously underrepresented in today's adult arts audience. Symphony orchestras, for example, find that their average ticket-buyer is over age 50.

Older citizens—those over 65—make up a full eighth of the total population. They have had less education to prepare them for an understanding of the arts, but they have more leisure time and interest in the arts. In addition, many enjoy more economic comfort than do the younger cohorts.

And there are the special audiences, strangers to most arts institutions because they belong to ethnic or linguistic subcultures or simply because they are among the full fifth of all adults who suffer temporarily or permanently from some disability of vision, hearing or mobility.

Programs must be devised to attract the attention of these diverse potential audiences—and to educate as well as entertain them. Adults must be reached where they are, at their work sites and in their communities. The classroom is not necessarily the most appropriate setting for adult arts education. Those potential audiences must be reached if, as taxpayers, they are to continue to provide even current levels of public support for arts institutions and if, as socializing agents, they are to pass on a commitment to the arts to upcoming generations.

This seminar attempts to define a new field: arts education for adults—its programs, problems and agendas. The constraints of time and limited resources precluded representation of every art form (the visual arts and museums are cited more often than theater, dance or the performing arts in general). Moreover, a disproportionate number of participants have begun the communication necessary to establish the field of adult arts education. They have begun to flesh out the exciting contents and institutional forms of arts education for adults and its future perspectives.

The pages that follow are the edited proceedings of the seminar. These are not formal academic papers, but rather, they are direct expressions of the experiences of individuals and institutions already active in this embryonic field. Collectively, they constitute a casebook, providing a sense of what is being done and how successfully it is being done, and addressing the questions and problems that remain to be tackled. They help us focus on the issues and provide a clearer agenda for tomorrow.

Participants include Samuel Lipman, publisher of *The New Criterion*, concert pianist, director of the Waterloo, New Jersey summer music festival and a strong advocate of quality arts education based upon works of acknowledged greatness. David Pankratz, a consultant in the field of arts education, reviews the literature and discusses the necessity and timeliness of concerted efforts to develop more sophisticated approaches to adult arts education.

They are followed by a panel discussing arts education in corporate and community settings. Katherine Niles, arts program director for PepsiCo, Inc., in Purchase, New York and Abby Remer, former director of art education at Chemical Bank in New York City, present the different rationales for the programs mounted by their respective corporations. Richard Clark, president, and Lynne Stoops, midwestern region residency manager, of Affiliate Artists, describe the success of this independent artist residency organization.

The panel on special audiences is composed of Paula Terry, Office of Special Constituencies in the National Endowment for the Arts, and Deborah Sonnenstrahl, associate professor of Art History/Museum Studies at Gallaudet University. They are joined by Ambrosia Shepard, poet and instructor in the Arts Mentor Program for the elderly in Washington, D.C. Collectively, they are concerned with redressing the neglect of special audiences — those with disabilities of hearing, sight or mobility — through public and private initiatives designed to increase access to arts institutions.

Museums have long conducted adult arts education. Not only is their experience central to an understanding of the issues, but these institutions provide educational models for other arts organizations, particularly those in the performing arts, which traditionally have not been concerned with educating their audiences. Participants here include Philip Yenawine, director of education for the Museum of Modern Art; Katherine Lochridge, former director of community education for the Metropolitan Museum of Art; and Thomas Newman, media specialist, also from the Metropolitan. Together they point up a variety of organizational problems: the inadequacy of knowledge about their varied publics, visual literacy of their audience, trade-offs between democratic and elite educational programs, uses and costs of new media technologies and pressures on museum organizations.

Broader questions about the potential of the mass media for arts education are addressed by Robert Kotlowitz, vice president for the arts and humanities at Channel 13/WNET. Here the focus shifts from the context of specific institutions to a consideration of widespread arts programming on television. Finally, Dale McConathy, chairperson of the Department of Art and Art Education at New York University, addresses the far-ranging sociocultural issues that influence the status and rootedness of the arts and adult education in our society.

If much work remains to establish the field of adult arts education, this casebook suggests valuable initial directions.

# ON ADULT ARTS EDUCATION

## by Samuel Lipman

The cycle of an ever-expanding arts audience in the United States is now coming to a close. All the information coming into the National Endowment for the Arts makes it clear that there has been a national leveling or even a decline in arts attendance, whether at opera companies, museums or symphony orchestras. Many people feel a decline is necessarily terrible. Regardless of whether it is, there is no doubt that it will have consequences—and one of these will be to push arts institutions into undertaking adult education, because they will see that this will provide them with any possibility of an audience at all. They are absolutely right about this, as they are about the likelihood that grant money for adult arts education will be available. So we are going to see more adult education in the arts.

The values of adult arts education are many. First, it provides a chance for adults—native born as well as immigrant—to make up what they have missed, what they never had the time or the opportunity to learn before. And that is important. Another side to adult arts education is that it gives us all a chance to make up for the mess we have made of arts education in general in this country. General arts education—not professional training—over the last 25 years has been abysmal, despite whatever statistics are presented to the contrary.

It is important now to clarify what adult arts education means. As a society, we had tended to expand, broaden and compromise the meaning of words so that they mean everything to everybody and, as a result, nothing to anybody. The three words *adult arts education* can easily lose any specific meaning and thus any specific content. What does the word *adult* include—or exclude? Is the opposite of *adult* arts education *children's* arts education? Does *adult arts education* exclude professional training? After all, most professional training is undertaken by people who are adult by any other understanding. Does it mean *nonstudent* education? If so, does that mean that

---

*Samuel Lipman is publisher of* The New Criterion. .

adult arts education has no real learning content? Do we mean instead *retraining?* No doubt many people pursue some kind of adult continuing education to change their lives, and this can be called retraining. By adult populations, do we otherwise mean the old, the seriously handicapped, those in hospitals and in prisons? Are they part of adult arts education too? If all these meanings are included, the field is enormously varied. By bringing all these meanings under the word *adult,* we are including much that we are not completely agreed upon, and the implications of which we do not understand.

What about the word *arts?* How should that be defined? When talking about the arts, everybody wants to speak for his or her own art. The problem is not only that of individuals, but also that of organized groups which have very serious stakes in the matter. The stakes are not purely artistic, of course: they involve self-definition, self-image, self-regard. And even if the problem of organized groups and their various interests can be overcome, we have to recognize that we live in a time when the very notion of "fine art" has become old-fashioned. When was the last time you heard anybody say "fine art"? It appears in museum titles occasionally, but in a historical context, it means a kind of rarefied elite activity. The society lost the prestige value of that in the 1960s and 1970s. We can no longer count on an automatic response in the population — positive or negative — to the term *fine art.* Perhaps we do not know ourselves what we mean by the term.

Finally, what do we mean by the word *education?* Is education to be what it was traditionally — teaching and learning? Or is education to be caring — a necessary caring — for client populations of various kinds? Are the art classes and music classes at senior citizens' centers *education?* Doubtless such classes are important for the people who come to them, and they fill important gaps in people's lives. But can we call this education? Do we create problems if we do? Learning centers of various types have courses, for example, in creative video games using personal computers. They also have movement classes. Is this arts education? Is this education at all? I would recommend against calling these activities education, but the pressures for doing so are high.

At present education remains "hot" in the nation's social and political climate, although we are on a downcurve. Washington's troubles over domestic and foreign policy have largely swamped the education debate. At the same time, people are still greatly concerned about what is happening to their children. Education in general, and arts education in particular, will profit from this concern. This necessarily includes adult arts education, which should not be split off from general arts education. Rather, the latter should be recognized as serving many populations, with possibly different needs, who may benefit from it.

How can we make sure that there will be benefits, that money will be well spent and that the people who undergo this education will be well served? We must start by letting adults be adults, the arts be the arts and education be education. This means treating the people who come into programs as adults, who are in large measure responsible for choosing to enter the program, are responsible for wanting to learn something and responsible for wanting to keep something after the class or the process is over.

We also have to be careful to let the arts be the arts. The goal of adult arts education has to be the ultimate communication of great works of art. There is a miracle about such works: they speak beyond the time when they were created and speak beyond the time when they are perceived. They speak beyond the person communicating them and beyond the person receiving them. They have a mystical life of their own. If that reality can be communicated in adult arts education, the students — or to use a more general term, the learners — will be left with a sense of the mystical experience of the great work of art. This experience can come only from great works of art. It cannot come from home-grown, loving-hands demonstrations. It has to come from the closest possible contact with greatness.

In addition, we have to try to teach something which can be tested in principle, if not readily in practice. Even mentioning the word *test* makes people nervous. It is not necessary for adult arts education to take place in classes in which grades are given. It is only that the teaching must have a firm curricular content. There is nothing wrong with having a curriculum and a program, with having structure, shape and discipline in education. Other than in rare charismatic situations, without such a structure, students end up with nothing.

Some knowledge of artistic practice may be a necessary first component. Those teaching music education should try to get people to read music. Those teaching the visual arts will find it much easier if the learners have already acquired rudimentary drawing skills. Wherever the teaching can start with something firm, in some sense, there will, in the long run, be more to show at the end.

Finally, in adult arts education — in any arts education — the primary concern is not with enhancing self-expression. Self-expression is appropriate as the outcome of learning, but learning has a difficult time if it is considered the outcome of self-expression. Much is known about teaching and learning, about curricula and about subject matter. But little is known about what self-expression is: it is different for everybody and it is different at every time for everybody. For these reasons, it cannot be the primary aim of any educational effort.

So what is adult arts education? It is people who want to learn about great art being taught by people who want to teach about great art. If this can be accomplished, our society will have gone a long way toward making up for past failures. Once, before the Second World War, we were better able to provide arts education in this country, although for a small and limited segment of the population. But clearly it *is* possible to do. What is required now is the will to provide it and the will to see that we are teaching art, that art is a part of civilization and that we are here to advance civilization. .

# ADULTS AND ARTS EDUCATION: A LITERATURE REVIEW

**by David B. Pankratz**

Unlike the research on K-12 art education or music education for young people, no discrete body of research exists on the topic of arts education for adults. Therefore, this literature review includes a wide variety of sources having implications for adult arts education, including writings on museum education, arts audience development, arts participation trends, arts and older adults, corporate art collections, recreation and the arts, broadcast media, adult education, arts councils, and the adult education programs of symphonies, opera companies, theaters and dance companies. (Limited space does not allow for consideration of university continuing education, labor education or architectural associations.) To supplement these sources, it has been necessary to gather information from many practitioners in arts education programs for adults, only a small portion of which can be represented here. The emphasis, therefore, will be on the literature itself, especially the critical literature.

The professional literature itself is not sophisticated in terms of social science methodology or policy analysis. Most writings have focused on logistics, program descriptions, broad justifications of education for adults and psychological accounts of adult learning characteristics. Few have dealt with sophisticated rationales for adult arts education, program development issues, fund development, the articulation of professional standards or the evaluation and analysis of program effects. Finally, interplay between practitioners and researchers has been slight. A reading of these sources suggests the broad conclusions that in educational settings the arts are a low priority, that in arts settings education is a low priority and that in almost all settings arts education for adults is a particularly low priority. The

*David B. Pankratz is a visiting researcher at Georgetown University and professorial lecturer in the Arts Management Program at American University, Washington, D.C.*

reasons for this state of affairs are many: a lack of perceived need for adult education in the arts, implicit goal conflicts such as elitism versus populism and creativity versus audience education, narrow views of arts marketing as opposed to long-term audience development, "cultural conservation" policies, limited funding and the lack of opportunities for professional development among practitioners. It must be stressed, however, that despite these constraints, many innovative arts education programs for adults do exist.

It is important to consider issues, problems and needs of adult arts education in various institutional settings, each of which has its own unique characteristics. The areas analyzed below include museum education, performing arts and adult education, arts education and older adults, arts education in nontraditional settings, and broadcast media.

## ART MUSEUMS AND ADULT EDUCATION

U.S. museums have a long history of offering adult education programs, dating back to an 1872 lecture series for adults by the Metropolitan Museum of Art.[1] Although throughout the twentieth century museum educators have given much greater attention to children than to adults, adult programs proliferated during the 1980s, at a faster rate than any other educational undertaking in museums. This trend was fueled in part by the influx of funds from the National Endowment for the Humanities and the National Endowment for the Arts during the 1960s and 1970s and by museums' recognition that adults are a greater source of revenue than are children, an attractive incentive in the fiscally tight 1980s.[2] Adult education programs, such as lecture series, individualized gallery talks, studio courses, film series, didactic exhibits, interpretive labels, discovery centers, detailed information sheets and a variety of audiovisual aids, appear in various combinations in almost every U.S. art museum. For example, as part of the extensive Kellogg Projects in Museum Education, the Toledo Museum of Art, through a museum communications consultant and its curatorial and educational staffs, devised new gallery introductions and a new system for writing labels as part of a museumwide commitment to public education.[3] The $150,000 Greek Vase Videodisc project of the J. Paul Getty Museum, consisting of stills, live-action segments, audio, and superimposed computer-text information on the Getty's Greek vases, is the first highly interactive computer-driven educational videodisc program implemented in a museum. At the High Museum of Art in Atlanta, lectures for adults on literature, philosophy, history, religion, popular culture and performing arts reflect the institution's move away from strictly art-historical approaches toward interdisciplinary programs designed to show the arts in their cultural contexts.

Despite these varied efforts, a 1984 American Association of Museums report, "Museums for a New Century," concluded that, in general, U.S. museums have yet to reach their educational potential. The report contends that many segments of the American public do not view museums as learning environments, that museums have no developed theory of the ideal nature of learning in museums and no overarching philosophy or philosophical framework for education in museums. The report argues that museums' educational activities have become largely auxiliary and intellectually isolated from their research and curatorial activities. Finally, the report presses for a renewed emphasis on the educational elements of museum galleries and exhibitions, which have been insufficiently exploited as educational resources. To stress this desirable new emphasis, the report coins the term "inreach" in contrast to outreach.

Contemporary critics, such as Albert William Levi and Nelson Goodman, have argued that museums have failed to clarify and distinguish their educational goals and purposes. Levi identifies three purposes that museums variously and often inconsistently serve: (1) to stimulate and direct aesthetic experiences; (2) to illuminate objects as reflective of their historical and cultural contexts; and (3) to present artworks as illustrating broad humanities themes.[4] Clearly advocating for aesthetic purpose, art educator Laura Chapman states that museum education should reconcile its misplaced trust in visitors' abilities to decipher the aesthetic codes of artworks and should inculcate ways of perceiving and thinking about art objects. Indeed, she sees museum education for adults as remedial education.[5]

But most of today's museum educators are aggressively egalitarian, attempting to meet the learning needs of all museum visitors at all levels of sophistication. For example, Patterson Williams of the Denver Art Museum contends that museum visitors are of secondary concern to museums and that, despite all the talk about outreach, museum professionals have failed to do all that they might to assist museum visitors in having excellent experiences with art objects.[6] In this spirit, the Denver Art Museum, in collaboration with the Arts Endowment and the J. Paul Getty Foundation, instituted a two-and-a-half-year experimental project designed to develop, produce, test and analyze practical exemplars of interpretive exhibitions to increase visitor satisfaction in museums. Based on studies of museum audiences — their diversity as well as their commonality of interests, levels of art knowledge, reading skills and attention spans — the project aims at inspiring the visitor's confidence in looking at artworks, in gaining personal meaning from them and in developing skills in making informed qualitative judgments. To develop a model of the ideal experience for museum visitors, the project will first study art experts' experience of art. Extensive interpretive materials will then be designed to help the visitor approximate the experience of the experts. On the basis of this project, the Denver Museum will revise its permanent collections over the next decade and, by disseminating the project's results, will provide a theoretical and practical model of public interpretation of art for the museum field.

## PERFORMING ARTS AND ADULT EDUCATION

The majority of American symphonies, opera companies and theaters, as well as some dance companies, offer adult education programs such as lecture series, preperformance talks, postperformance discussions, membership newsletters, extended program notes and cooperative programs with educational institutions. Many of these programs are undertaken on a break-even budget and administered largely by volunteers. In contrast to museum education, there is almost no written professional literature on the topic, not even program descriptions, let alone philosophical debates or calls for more research.

For symphonies, adult education programs seem to be activated by an interest in enhancing the concert experience of symphony subscribers or in "building" new audiences.[7] As an American Symphony Orchestra League chairman said, "People are out there in sufficient numbers to join us in a search for a memorable tune."[8] The Chicago Symphony Women's Association, as a notable example, has sponsored evening programs with contemporary composers whose works are receiving Chicago premieres, preconcert talks by conductors or soloists, and all-day seminars, some in collaboration with the Art Institute of Chicago, on such broad themes as romanticism and expressionism in art and music.

Adult education programs in opera, according to a recent survey by OPERA America, assist companies in retaining audiences and in improving the aesthetic decision-making skills of program participants.[9] For example, the Houston Grand Opera offers cooperative university-based continuing education programs on operas to be performed during the season, extensive preperformance lectures, preview discussions in local libraries and booklets with extensive information on the season's operas, mailed to subscribers before each production.

Several adult education programs in the theater are noteworthy. The

Omaha Magic Theatre presents many postplay dialogues, often led by humanities scholars, on issues presented in contemporary plays. The Actors Theatre of Louisville's Classics in Context festivals present films, lectures and printed materials designed to give audiences a broader perspective on the social, political and artistic influences surrounding the creation of selected plays. The multifaceted Alabama Shakespeare Festival's Theatre in the Mind project is designed to foster audience awareness in theater as a mode of thought, a repository of human values and a means of comprehending American culture as well as other cultures and other eras. Finally, the Oregon Shakespeare Festival, among its many adult education activities, offers elderhostel classes for older adults, taught by the Festival's artistic and administrative staff.

Presenters of the performing arts are often constrained in their presentation of in-depth adult education programs because of the short stays of touring artists and companies. Despite these constraints, the University of Iowa's Hancher Auditorium presents an extensive array of preperformance lectures, demonstrations and symposia on contemporary artists and on humanities and social themes of theater productions, along with postperformance discussions.

A major work in the field by Bradley G. Morison and Julie G. Dalgleish, *Waiting in the Wings: A Larger Audience for the Arts,* places the adult education programs of performing arts organizations in a new context.[10] The authors note that, although attendance at performing arts events has increased in recent decades, the demographic reach of performing arts organizations has not expanded. They contend that as the growth of younger, professional, well-educated arts audiences declines, performing arts organizations will require sophisticated programs combining marketing and educational elements. They further contend that, although some adult education programs are unarguably excellent, they are rarely integral to the audience development needs of arts organizations and are tantamount to preaching to the converted. Performing arts organizations, to date, have become overreliant on dynamic subscription promotion (DSP) campaigns, which advocate a hard-sell approach to arts marketing, stress snob appeal and assume that once people are in their seats they will understand and enjoy the performances and then return. Also, the popular Stanford Research Institute's Values and Lifestyles System (VALS), which claims to be a "fresh approach to understanding why people act as they do as consumers and as social human beings," is criticized as being a mere variation on long-accepted basic principles of selling, holding little promise for broadening the demographic reach of arts audiences.[11] Morison and Dalgleish argue for a step-by-step audience development process, labeled

SELL (Strategy to Encourage Lifelong Learning), in which arts organizations would offer accessible point-of-entry series to potential new audiences, leading to increasingly more sophisticated offerings. Throughout the process, arts programs would be augmented by educational programs and materials. *Waiting in the Wings* will likely stimulate much thinking about adult education programs within performing arts organizations.

## ARTS EDUCATION AND OLDER ADULTS

The literature on arts education and older adults is prodigious, much of it published by the Center for Arts and Aging of the National Council on Aging (NCOA), which has served as an informational center and advocate for the arts and aging since 1973.

Recurrent concerns in the field of the arts and aging are the needs for preservice and inservice training and for increased financial commitment to arts programs by aging agencies as well as public arts agencies. A curious feature of the literature is that, whereas writers point out that only a small minority of older adults reside in institutional settings, the majority of writings in the field deal with arts programs in institutional settings.[12]

The literature deals with two general forms of arts education for older adults — creative expression and arts audience development. Writers on the arts and aging agree that the creative arts uniquely can provide a voice for older adults to articulate their needs, desires and aspirations, contributing to their mental health and personal integration.[13] Research shows that older adults' creativity does not diminish with age; contrary to popular images, 90 percent of the elderly can engage in creative activity. NCOA publications detail many programs which foster creativity as opposed to prepackaged arts kits used merely to fill time. Moreover, some argue that although creative experiences are valuable for older adults, older adults can and should be additionally educated to perceive and study the arts with critical eyes.[14]

On audience education and older adults, research shows that despite increased attendance at arts events, older adults are still underrepresented in arts audiences. Factors such as cost, transportation and lack of availability are perceived as barriers to attendance.[15] In a 1975 University of Wisconsin study, arts administrators were found to be largely uninterested in nurturing audience development among older adults.[16] In part this was because they felt the elderly were difficult to define as an audience segment and in part because educational programs for younger persons were more cost-effective, with young people representing potential audiences for many years to come. In recent years, attitudes have changed somewhat. As one example, the Krannert Center for the Performing Arts at the University of Illinois has devised a senior adults program with special events, newsletters, accessible transportation, a hearing amplification system and a liaison staff member.[17]

## ARTS EDUCATION IN NONTRADITIONAL SETTINGS

An obvious example of arts education in nontraditional settings is Affiliate Artists, which is discussed in depth later in this volume. Another example is Arts in the Marketplace, a program sponsored by the Rouse Company. For close to a decade, the program has sponsored artist residencies, workshops, performances and art exhibitions in museum branches in many of its retail centers, all of which are designed to entertain shoppers while maintaining a subtle educational emphasis.[18] The long-term effect of such programs, in educational terms, has not been documented.

Art collections in private U.S. corporations today number about 800.[19] Yet writers in *The Corporate Art Report,* a now-defunct journal, argued that too many corporate art collections missed obvious opportunities for employee education in the arts.[20] Suggestions included identification labels, slides, tours, videotape presentations, in-house publications, copies of reviews, and lunchtime seminars. Even where they exist, these efforts have yet to be documented. Corporate-sponsored branch museums housed in public areas of corporate office buildings, such as the Whitney branches in New York City, have an avowedly educational purpose in developing interest in art among both employees and passersby who visit the building. However, Thomas Armstrong of the Whitney has questioned whether branch museums can be replicated except in large urban centers.[21] Also, research has not yet shown clearly whether visits to branch museums even stimulate attendance at other museums.

Many view art classes in parks and recreation facilities, YMCAs, YWCAs and Jewish community centers as opportunities to introduce adults to the arts in accessible environments, at their own pace and level of interest and in a relaxed manner.[22] Although activity in these settings would seem to be great, few evaluation studies or even statistics are available. Generally, these programs are heavily weighted toward studio arts classes designed to elicit creative expression. One study of community art education classes in an Oregon community, conducted by art educator Rogena Degge, concluded that the artist-teachers there were well qualified and certified to teach art; whether these standards are met in other community settings has yet to be studied.

## BROADCAST MEDIA

Critics of television frequently lament that the promise of television to elevate public tastes has been unfulfilled. Despite these criticisms, a recent Arts Endowment study on participation in the arts has shown that far more people experience the performing arts through television than through live events.[23] The study also concludes that the media are not an alternative but a supplement and perhaps a stimulant to attendance at live performances.

However, the promise of cable television as an educational tool for the arts has remained unfulfilled. A nonprofit arts cable network — PACE — proposed by a Carnegie Commission and designed to introduce different publics to the arts according to their levels of experience never materialized.[24] A Corporation for Public Broadcasting (CPB) study concludes that advances in cable television occur more as a result of engineering developments than as a result of an identification of audience needs.[25] Because of the failure of cable arts stations, CPB concludes that it has had fewer opportunities for creative collaborations on educational arts programming.[25]

## GENERAL ISSUES

Several issues cut across all of the areas discussed above. One obvious concern is funding. For years, the Arts Endowment has stressed the importance of programs promoting access to the arts. But by its own account, as its recent five-year plan noted, "It is in many ways easier to assist artists and arts institutions; we have done much less, specifically, to assist the process of reaching new discerning audiences. We have not yet developed comprehensive strategies to broaden audiences geographically and demographically."[27]

As for the private sector, Paul DiMaggio, in his analysis of the role of the marketplace in the art world, argues that the market does not support the notion of access to the arts as a priority.[28] Defining educational access to the arts as a purpose without a market, he argues that the issue of increased access must be addressed in a variety of forms by foundation donors.[29] DiMaggio notes, however, that efforts to encourage support for adult arts education are damaged by the lack of infrastructure to synchronize such efforts and the lack of research on programs that effectively promote increased participation in the arts.

Another key question, of course, is where the needed research on adult arts education is going to come from. Marylou Kuhn and, more recently, James Hutchens, among other arts educators, have advocated increased interest in lifelong learning in the arts among arts education researchers. Response, however, has been limited. Unfortunately, adult arts education in community settings is often viewed as an unserious, spare-time activity, not worthy of investigation by arts educators still tied to a schoolhouse view of arts education.[30] For different reasons, sociologists and political scientists have yet to look at issues in adult arts education. Finally, adult education researchers have contributed the popular idea of "androgogy," a concept of some influence for museum educators.[31] Variously described as a theory of adult learning and a prescription for adult education practice, androgogy holds that adult learning is self-directed and task- or problem-centered; it develops from life tasks and is motivated by internal incentives. In line with this view, it has been argued that cultural institutions should foster independent, self-directed learning by a process of mediation designed to meet adults' learning needs.[32] Others have contended, however, that adult educators are not obliged to consider adults' expressions of learning needs as the sole criterion for adult program development.[33]

Adult arts education must also be viewed in light of cultural policy issues. One of those issues is whether public funds should be used to assist adults in experiencing the arts of high culture. Some have argued that it is not justified and that other cultures of equal social and aesthetic value should receive public support.[34] Radical adult educators argue that high culture is at best irrelevant and at worst oppressive to various social classes. In their view the ideal role of adult education is to foster among oppressed communities critical voices challenging the dominant culture, a goal that is furthered by participatory creation of socially meaningful artworks.[35] These issues have received some discussion, especially in Britain, but more is needed.[36]

Finally, opportunities for professional development among adult arts education practitioners, particularly across disciplinary lines, have thus far been limited. To develop a truly comprehensive endeavor, based on an effective relationship between theory and practice, more extensive opportunities for cross-fertilization must be provided. This seminar is thus a beginning along these lines.

## NOTES

1. Barbara Y. Newsom and Adele Z. Silver, eds., *The Art Museum as Educator* (Berkeley, Calif.: University of California Press, 1987).

2. Barbara Y. Newsom, "A Decade of Uncertainty for Museum Educators," *Museum News* 58, no. 5 (May/June 1980): 46-50.

3. Mary Ellen Munley, *Catalysts for Change: The Kellogg Projects in Museum Education* (Washington, D.C.: The Kellogg Projects in Museum Education, 1986).

4. Albert William Levi, "The Art Museum as an Agency of Culture," *Journal of Aesthetic Education* 19, no. 2 (Summer 1985): 23-40 and Nelson Goodman, "The End of the Museum?" *Journal of Aesthetic Education* 19 no. 2 (Summer 1985): 53-62.

5. Laura Chapman, "The Future and Museum Educators," *Museum News* 60, no. 6 (July/August 1982): 48-56.

6. Patterson B. Williams, "Educational Excellence in Art Museums: An Agenda for Reform," *Journal of Aesthetic Education,* 19, no. 2 (Summer 1985): 105-23.

7. Joseph Truskot, Anita Belofsky and Karen Kittilstad, *Orchestra Education Programs: A Handbook and Directory of Education and Outreach Programs* (Washington, D.C.: American Symphony Orchestra League, 1984).

8. Matthew Sigman, "Building New Audiences," *Symphony Magazine,* 36, no. 4 (August/September 1985): 36-37.

9. OPERA America, "Adult Education: 1985 Survey Results and Program Examples," *Working Ideas* (Washington, D.C.: OPERA America, 1985).

10. Bradley G. Morison and Julie Gordon Dalgleish, *Waiting in the Wings: A Larger Audience for the Arts and How to Develop It* (New York: American Council for the Arts, 1987).

11. Ibid.

12. As for the literature itself, Jean Ellen Jones contends that writings in the field are largely descriptive and that the field is in great need of theoretical work to define its territory and experimental designs comparing program designs and effects. Jean Ellen Jones, guest editor, "Older Americans and the Arts," *Educational Gerontology* 8, no. 2 (1982).

13. Nadia Weisberg and Rosilyn Wilder, eds., *Creative Arts with Older Adults* (New York: Human Sciences Press, 1985).

14. Pearl Greenberg, *Visual Arts and Older People: Developing Quality Programs* (Springfield, Ill.: Charles C. Thomas, Publisher, 1987).

15. John P. Robinson, *Cultural Participation in the Arts. Final Report on the 1985 Survey,* vol. 1 (Washington, D.C.: National Endowment for the Arts, 1986).

16. Alton C. Johnson, et al., *Older Americans: The Unrealized Audience for*

the Arts (Madison, Wis.: Center for Arts Administration, University of Wisconsin, 1975).

17. Priscilla McCutcheon, *Developing Older Audiences: Guidelines for Performing Arts Groups* (Washington, D.C.: The National Council on Aging, Inc., 1985).

18. Becky Hannum, ed., *Art in the Marketplace* (Columbia, Md.: The Rouse Company, 1984).

19. Shirley Reiff Howarth, ed., *Directory of Corporate Art Collections* (Largo, Fla.: International Art Alliance, 1984).

20. Randy Rosen, "Education: The New Frontier in Corporate Art," *Corporate Art Report* 2, no. 1 (March/April 1984): 2; and Lynn Sowder, "Education as Part of the Corporate Art Program," *Corporate Art Report* 1, no. 3 (July/August 1983): 4.

21. William Keens, interviewer, "Serving Up Culture: The Whitney and Its Branch Museums," *Museum News* 64, no. 4 (April 1986): 22-28.

22. Barry D. Mangum, "Challenges and Possibilities in Arts Programming," *Parks and Recreation* 14, no. 7 (July 1979): 24-27; and "A Giant Step Forward for the Arts in Leisure," *Parks and Recreation* 17, no. 7 (July 1982): 30-32.

23. John P. Robinson, *Cultural Participation in the Arts Final Report on the 1985 Survey.* Vol I prepared for the Research Division, National Endowment for the Arts. Washington, D. C.: National Endowment for the Arts, 1986.

24. Sheila Mahoney, Nick DeMartino and Robert Stengel, *Keeping PACE With the New Television: Public Television and Changing Technology* (New York, N.Y.: The Carnegie Corporation, UNU Books International, 1980).

25. John Carey, *Telecommunications Technologies and Public Broadcasting* (Washington, D.C.: Corporation for Public Broadcasting, 1986).

26. Ibid.

27. National Endowment for the Arts, *Five-Year Plan, 1986-1990* (Washington, D.C.: National Endowment for the Arts, 1984): 124.

28. Paul J. DiMaggio, "The Nonprofit Instrument and the Influence of the Marketplace on Policies in the Arts," in W. McNeil Lowry, ed., *The Arts and Public Policy in the United States* (Englewood Cliffs, N.J.: Prentice-Hall, Inc., 1984).

29. Paul J. DiMaggio, *The Role of Independent Foundation in the Arts,* Report to the Ford Foundation, September, 1985.

30. Katherine Brown, "Turning a Poor Relative into a Rich Relative," *Art Education* 36, no. 1: 36-37.

31. Zipporah W. Collins, ed., *Museums, Adults, and the Humanities: A Guide to Educational Programming* (Washington, D.C.: American Association of Museums, 1981).

32. David Carr, "Self-Directed Learning in Cultural Institutions," in *Self-Directed Learning: From Theory to Practice,* edited by Stephen Brookfield, New Directions for Continuing Education 25 (San Francisco: Jossey-Bass Publishers, March 1985): 51-62, and "Mediation as a Helping Presence in Cultural Institutions," in *Involving Adults in the Educational Process,* edited by S.H. Rosenblum, New Directions for Continuing Education 26 (San Francisco, Jossey-Bass Publishers, June 1985): 87-96.

33. Stephen D. Brookfield, *Understanding and Facilitating Adult Learning* (San Francisco: Jossey-Bass Publishers, 1986).

34. Herbert J. Gans, *Popular Culture and High Culture: An Analysis and Evaluation of Taste* (New York: Basic Books, Inc., 1974).

35. Owen Kelley, *Community, Art and the State: Storming the Citadels* (London: Comedia Publishing, 1984).

36. Richard Hoggart, *An English Temper* (New York: Oxford University Press, 1982).

# ARTS EDUCATION IN

## corporate and community settings

# ARTS EDUCATION IN CORPORATE AND COMMUNITY SETTINGS

Corporate support of the arts, though long-standing in the United States, has taken a huge leap since the 1960s. From a total of $22 million at that time, corporate arts philanthropy has risen to more than $700 million in 1987, outpacing increased government allocations, $165 million from the National Endowment for the Arts and $212 million from various state arts agencies in 1987, as well as foundation grants. Collectively, these sources of support for the arts contribute about a third of the total national expenses of nonprofit arts organizations.

Corporations support the arts in a number of ways. They underwrite exhibitions and performances; they have memberships in arts organizations; they donate gifts and they cooperate in sponsoring special programs, promoting community arts programs, etc. Many have established substantial art collections of their own. According to the Business Committee for the Arts, more than 800 corporations now collect art, an increase of more than 50 percent in the total number of such collections since 1980.

Corporations view support of the arts as good business and as enlightened self-interest. Support has been justified as an excellent form of public relations, as a good investment, as a form of social responsibility and as a means of providing an enhanced "quality of life" for employees, clients and community neighbors.

Yet, despite growing patronage, most corporations have not yet found an impetus for arts education programs. Only recently have some corporations begun to include an explicit educational component in their arts programs. The educational imperative is beginning to be seen as a natural and necessary extension of the growing presence of the arts and of a public with expanding interest and leisure time, eager to know more about the arts.

The specific nature of corporate arts education programs and the degree of their success are contingent upon a number of variables, such as the nature of the business (financial, manufacturing, service); its location (New York City or Pocatello, Idaho); the educational and socioeconomic distribution of its employees; its clientele (local, national or international); and the internal structuring of its arts programs (controlled by the chief executive officer or delegated to a professional arts staff).

Katherine F. Niles, arts program director for PepsiCo Inc., provides one example. PepsiCo's internationally known sculpture garden at its corporate headquarters in exurban Purchase, New York is actively shared with the neighboring community as well as with its employees and clients. PepsiCo's efforts in arts education are largely informal and nondidactic.

A more formal and sequential arts educational program is provided by Chemical Bank, under Abby Remer, former director of arts education. Situated in Manhattan, Chemical is also able to sponsor collaborative programs with art museums.

In contrast to corporate arts educational efforts enacted in settings that have a relatively consistent available audience is the Affiliate Artists residency program. Richard Clark, president, and Lynne Stoops, mid-western region residency manager, describe how Affiliate Artists brings highly qualified performing artists from a variety of disciplines into local communities, using local corporate sponsors and local presenting agencies. The Informance, a unique educational tool, is the means by which Affiliate Artists engages community audiences.

These are three successful programs. Yet it is obvious that the field of corporate and community-based adult arts education is still in its infancy. Not only do efforts need to be augmented but they also need to be under-stood. For instance, there are no comparative or longitudinal studies demonstrating conclusively that artists' residencies or on-site corporate arts collections and docent programs lead to lifetime arts participation. Nor is much known about the effects of arts programs directed by chief executive officers versus those of a more institutionalized approach to arts program-ming. Will only noncontroversial and established art receive corporate sup-port, thus serving disproportionately as the basis for corporate arts education programs? There are insufficient data on a variety of collabora-tive ventures among corporate and arts educational institutions to know what the successes have been and where the pitfalls may lie. Though the answers are not clear, at least the questions are beginning to be asked.

# PEPSICO SCULPTURE GARDENS

## by Katherine F. Niles

Corporations today influence our sensibilities in many ways through marketing and promotion. Some corporations, including PepsiCo, Inc., contribute to a variety of social and educational programs, including those in the arts. They believe they have a responsibility to improve the quality of life in their communities and, indeed, in the world.

PepsiCo's undertakings in the arts are long-standing. In 1970 PepsiCo opened its world headquarters in then-rural Purchase, New York on a "campus" of 114 acres. Chief Executive Officer Donald M. Kendall believed that such an environment would enhance both physical and cultural "fitness" activities for employees. He selected Edward Durrell Stone as architect, mandating that the design for the headquarters integrate three art forms: architecture, landscape architecture and large-scale sculpture. An arboretum and botanical garden were established, and a collection of sculpture was begun through direct commission or selection of work undertaken by Kendall himself. That collection now totals 40 pieces, including works by Auguste Rodin, Alexander Calder, Jacques Lipchitz, Arnaldo Pomodoro, Henry Moore, Isamu Noguchi, Louise Nevelson, Claes Oldenburg and David Smith. In its garden setting, it is literally a museum without walls.

PepsiCo's arts audience goes well beyond its employees. The community's enthusiastic response to the sculpture gardens prompted Kendall to keep the gardens open to the public every day of the year, at no charge. Thus there are two publics for this art collection: one is composed of company employees, the other is composed of visitors — both those who have business to conduct at PepsiCo and those who are in the neighborhood. Pepsico has more than 10,000 visitors annually. For those who come to stroll in the gardens, maps and lists of the sculpture are provided, including information on the artists and the titles and dates of the pieces. From

*Katherine F. Niles is director of the arts program at PepsiCo, Inc.*

that, the viewer can derive a more educated experience in walking through the gardens. During the summer, an information center operates in the gardens. A catalog, available to the public and to employees upon request, has pictures and a description of each piece in the collection, along with a review essay explaining PepsiCo's interest in its art collection. Many catalogs are distributed by executives in recruiting new employees and in meeting international visitors.

A film called *A Century Crystalized,* which relates the sculpture collection to other art of the twentieth century, was produced to broaden the company's educational efforts and help place the artworks in a wider artistic context. The film is shown on request to groups when they visit the gardens, as no formal docent program exists. The film is also in national circulation, distributed free to art schools, colleges and cable television companies.

There is no compulsory or specialized program of arts education for employees. Rather, the company provides opportunities for the discovery of new art forms and the repeated experiences of viewing them. Interest in learning about the sculpture varies among employees as much as it does among the general population. When a major new piece is being installed, however, the artist is, in effect, "in residence." Informally—and sometimes formally through a lecture—the artist helps to educate employees about the work's aesthetic. Over the years, formal lecture series have been conducted for employees and others—at present, for the wives of top and middle-management executives. These women often play the role of "ambassadors" in the community, and accordingly, they are frequently asked about the sculpture gardens. Although some may have originally attended the lecture series because of that community role, many now want to learn more out of an increasing interest in and excitement about modern art. As a result, this and some of Pepsico's other lecture series have become springboards for employee group visits to the Guggenheim and other museums.

In addition to the sculpture gardens, PepsiCo sponsors a much-acclaimed international performing arts festival, Summerfare, on the campus of the State University of New York at Purchase, about a mile away. Both classics and contemporary works are performed by new and well-established companies. As with the sculpture gardens, any arts education is indirect and subtle, based on the belief that appreciation comes through repeated exposure rather than through direct programs.

Neither the sculpture collection nor Summerfare is intended as a promotional or public relations tool for PepsiCo itself. The company's goal has been to provide a rich and continuing experience of art of the highest quality, in the workplace and the community. In meeting that goal, PepsiCo has contributed to the arts education of large numbers of people.

# THE EMERGENCE OF ART EDUCATION IN THE WORKPLACE: CHEMICAL BANK'S PROGRAM

**by Abby Remer**

Art education is not yet widely accepted as vital to a sophisticated corporate art program. However, without an accompanying education program, any collection — no matter how wonderful — merely hangs on the walls as decoration.

Art education programs encourage participants to examine and eventually to feel comfortable with the natural diversity which exists in our society. By teaching visual literacy skills, education programs enhance viewers' abilities to comprehend ideas and express themselves. The result is often vigorous discussion among viewers which contributes to a more innovative working atmosphere. The sterility of the workplace is broken by the lively discussion of ideas that art promotes. As educator and writer Harold Rosenberg once stated, "A great work of art is a work of art about which people can differ widely and yet be right."

## EVOLUTION OF THE PROGRAM

Chemical Bank's art collection, established in 1981, consists of more than 1,700 works, primarily by American artists, with an emphasis on work done in the 1980s. The Arts Program consists of two permanent in-house staff — the art administrator and the director of art education — working with two consultants who acquire the fine art and fine art posters. Two additional consultants assist with installations and maintenance of the collection.

Chemical's Education Program was established as an integral part of the

---

*Abby Remer is a consultant to corporations on corporate art education programs and is the former director of art education at Chemical Bank.*

Art Program. The first goal of the Education Program was to make the Bank's collection accessible to a wider audience. A second goal was to foster a greater understanding of contemporary art among the employees who were surrounded by the works on a daily basis. This understanding was to be accomplished through a third goal, which was to cultivate basic visual literacy skills. Educational programs were created for the Bank's three major constituencies—employees, clients and the general public. After the goals were identified, a second major stage took place in the development of the Education Program—that of long-term planning. A cohesive series of programs was envisioned to continually provide introductory experiences while simultaneously offering more sophisticated programs for previous participants. A brief chronology of the first two years of the Education Program follows.

Before even submitting a proposal, the art administrator and director of art education surveyed existing art education programs for 30 corporate collections across the country. On the basis of the survey a one-year plan was outlined and submitted to other personnel in the Administration Unit, whose ideas and reactions to the proposal were incorporated into the program. Such a procedure cultivated support and understanding of the Education Program from the start.

The first activity in the Education Program was a walking tour of the third- and fourth-floor galleries at the world headquarters building. The tour included a talk about the Bank's rationale for collecting art, gave information about each work viewed and provided participants with an introduction to basic visual literacy. To promote cooperation from the start of the Educational Program, departments in the Bank were invited to attend special walking tours. After these specially-conducted programs, the walking tour was offered to all Chemical Bank employees through an announcement in the in-house newsletter. During the first three months more than 100 employees from all levels of the Bank—from tellers to managing directors—at more than 21 locations took part in the tour. To cultivate an even wider audience for the Bank's activities, the tours were expanded in the summer of 1987 to include clients and guests of employees.

The next activity established was Wednesday noontime talks in the Chemical Gallery. Because the gallery is located in the lobby of the world headquarters building, this program reaches beyond employees. The exhibitions, accompanied by explanatory labels and color brochures, showcase art from the Bank's collection. The second-floor Highlights Gallery—on the most traveled floor of the Bank—exhibits a few works in alcoves. This Gallery's exhibits always include large explanatory texts next to each artwork and are correlated to the theme of the downstairs gallery exhibition.

From the outset, older programs, such as tours for students of art or arts administration, museum members, or outside professional groups, were integrated into the Education Program's schedule, as were loans to art institutions and a student internship program.

Once the initial activities were under way, participants from the walking tours were surveyed about three alternative future programs. The program overwhelmingly preferred by employees was conducted in two sessions: the first part took place at the Museum of Modern Art, where employees explored major art trends from 1930 to 1970, which provided them with a background to view the Bank's contemporary collection during the second session. The program, accommodating 25 participants, was conducted twice with waiting lists of more than 80 people.

## NEW DIRECTIONS

Several new programs are now being established. Different areas of the Bank are being explored during walking tours to expose the participants to more of the collection. To provide information when personnel from the Art Administration Unit are unavailable, individual art information booklets and self-guided walking tours are being created for distribution to employees and clients by receptionists. The booklets contain biographies of the artists and information on each artwork. The self-guiding tour includes a map and brief essays on the art in a selected area.

Another activity being initiated is informal after-installation talks which will provide information on artworks and the rationale for the Bank's collection. This format will allow questions to be immediately addressed, and employees will be encouraged to attend more of the Education Program's activities.

The Education Program has entered a more sophisticated stage whereby collaboration is being fostered with other departments of the Bank and with outside institutions. At present, through a collaboration with the Corporate Social Policy Division, which manages philanthropy, a program is being devised to serve schools, senior-citizen centers, and museums in which Chemical is a corporate member. This program, also in two parts, begins with on-site slide presentations to these groups, using the Bank's collection to discuss contemporary art and to develop visual literacy skills; the second part consists of guided group visits to a museum.

Another collaborative effort of the Bank, in partnership with an East Village gallery and The New Museum of Contemporary Art, has produced a three-session program covering the Bank's collection and its acquisition procedures, the gallery's function and relationship to corporations, and a visit to The New Museum that includes a discussion of the museum's relationship to galleries, artists and corporations. Both inside and outside the Bank, immense excitement has been generated by the sharing of these resources.

## CONTRIBUTORS TO SUCCESS

Why have these corporate art education programs succeeded? A number of tangential elements, though not necessarily conclusive, are worth looking at. For one, the banking industry is in the midst of deregulation and hence is rapidly changing. To stay ahead in business, employees must be open to, and indeed help to create, change. The question is, are these people more accepting or interested in the new and challenging ideas of art (particularly contemporary art) than people in other industries? Though no means are available to test this idea, it is worth pondering. Location may also be a factor. If a corporation is in the midst of a large metropolitan center, are employees more or less apt to demonstrate an interest in art? From experience, it appears that despite the multitude of cultural resources available in urban areas, many employees feel somewhat intimidated in approaching art or art institutions on their own. When art educators in a corporation offer a comfortable learning environment, either on the premises or at museums and galleries, employees flock to the events. Moreover, a collection and its related education programs may have an easier time gaining democratic acceptance if they are not closely identified with the chief executive officer or other senior officer. Acceptance is likely to be greater when employees attend solely out of their own interests. There is nothing political to gain since attendance at the programs was not "suggested" by a higher authority. The programs also attract lower level employees, which they might not do were they sponsored by senior management.

How does the type of art in a collection affect the number of participants in education programs? If 84 percent of corporate collections consist of contemporary art, then a great part of the work force has had no formal introduction to this type of art before. Even if people have studied art in school, the curricula rarely cover contemporary art. If anything, viewers have studied the "old masters" and are confused by the contemporary art that surrounds them. The art-educated "yuppie" generation seems to have been schooled in the classics and has little frame of reference for contemporary art. Furthermore, contemporary art by nature can arouse a defensive response from people who feel they do not "understand" it. Hence, those who are exposed to contemporary art at the workplace may be more apt to attend education programs, because these programs offer viewers an opportunity to combat their uncomfortable feeling of being naive about art. Tellingly, after programs have been conducted, quite a few employees have mentioned that they no longer feel "dumb" about art and that they feel confident in discussing their reactions with others.

Two undoubted contributors to the success of the Art Education Program have already been mentioned. One was the ability to establish from the beginning a cohesive long-range plan that meshed with the general goals of the Art Program. The other factor is continual internal and external collaboration. A third important contributor is the means employed to educate participants. The programs rely largely on the person-to-person mode of teaching, the most effective method of education. In this method, programs can be adapted to a particular participant's needs. Person-to-person programs also provide a forum whereby answers and ideas can be solicited from the audience. This proactive method of learning ensures better integration of the material; it also instills a sense of pride in the participants for their contribution to the learning process. In addition, soliciting ideas from participants prompts them to examine their expectations of art. This process helps them become receptive to developing an understanding and an ability to enjoy art, thereby moving them away from immediate judgments, such as "I like this work," or "I don't like this work." The last element in the Education Program's success is the Bank's decision to devote staff time to its development and implementation. This raises an important point—the necessity of recognition for the emerging field of art education in the workplace. Not only do personnel need to allocate time to this vital aspect of an art program, but serious and thorough art education training must take place. As art educators, curators and administrators become active educators, they must take a serious look at the issues. For instance, where will the training come from? Communication skills can be learned from good art educators in museum or academic settings. Yet these models should not be wholly incorporated into the corporate setting. The audiences in these two environments come with vastly different expectations, and the modes of teaching must reflect this fact. As previously mentioned, an interactive process in which ideas are solicited from participants is one of the most effective educational methods, and one more apt to suit the needs of a corporate audience. In an academic or museum setting, individuals come with expectations of passively being taught by the "experts."

At work, however, employees actively collaborate with their colleagues and supervisors to get tasks accomplished. Why should these same adults suddenly be asked, or allowed, to stop participating during their experiences with art? The answer is that they should not. Methods of training educators to facilitate this kind of participation need to be developed.

The field must also address, just as individual corporations must, the role, definition and goals of art education in the workplace.

Lastly, for art education in the workplace to progress as a field, people must start to communicate with one another. Sharing resources, ideas and experiences is the only way to prevent isolated individuals from "discovering the wheel" separately. Only through collaboration in its truest sense can art education in the workplace move forward. As this new field emerges and begins to establish itself with cohesive long-range plans, quality educational training, collaboration and a sharing of experiences, it is imperative to remember that individuals and art education itself will have to evolve constantly to meet the growing needs and expanded knowledge of the audience. Art education, like ideas about art itself, should never be carved in stone.

# AFFILIATE ARTISTS

## by Richard C. Clark and Lynne Stoops

Affiliate Artists, now 20 years old, was established primarily to find new employment opportunities for the nation's most talented young performing artists. The program arose in the mid-1960s, when most American singers were working in the opera houses of Western Europe — for America, a tremendous waste of a national resource. Affiliate Artists was set up to help reverse the traffic, to put the nation's best performers into U.S. communities. The assumption was that every American was a potential participant in an audience and a potential supporter of the arts. The founders of Affiliate Artists also believed that the arts and the artists of this country need the support of all citizens, not just 3 or 4 percent of the population.

By 1966 the corporate community was a potential resource of critical importance to the arts. Enlightened corporate leaders at the Sears-Roebuck Foundation responded sympathetically in 1969 to Affiliate Artists' formulation of the problem of creating performance opportunities for American artists. Since then more than 70 large and mid-size corporations have invested in the cultural life of the nation and its communities through Affiliate Artists programs.

Affiliate Artists' primary vehicle is the "residency," through which a solo professional performer is placed in a U.S. community, sponsored by a corporation or other institution in collaboration with a local presenting organization. The artist performs for a cross section of the population — wherever people gather to work, study or socialize. During a residency of up to several weeks the artist gives two performances, called "Informances," daily in settings such as offices, factories, service clubs and schools. The artist not only performs but also talks with the audience about his or her life, career and craft. The artist is thus both building bridges to the audience and eliminating the invisible "fourth wall" of the traditional con-

*Richard C. Clark is president of Affiliate Artists. Lynne Stoops is residency manager of Affiliate Artists' midwestern region.*

cert or theater stage, thereby strengthening the local arts presenting organization's link to a much broader section of the community.

Over the last 20 years more than 350 artists have given Informances — some 3,500 a year — in a total of 9,000 residency weeks. Artists are selected following highly competitive auditions for five-year fellowships as Affiliate Artists. They spend considerable time with experienced consultants, most of them alumni, to perfect the special communication and "people" skills essential for this type of work. These same skills are transferable to almost every other aspect of their professional careers.

Affiliate Artists staff match these individual performers with corporate sponsors who wish to fund a local residency and with a local presenting organization which sets up the specific program schedule. The latter organization is selected with great care after thorough research by Affiliate Artists personnel into the community's resources. It may be an orchestra, an arts council or a producing organization; it must be organization that can adopt Affiliate Artists' vision of community outreach and use the program to make people excited about the arts. The presenter must make a commitment to the spirit of the program and have the staff and resources necessary to make the program work. Affiliate Artists provides a handbook and on-site training encouraging the presenter.to use the artist's visits as a hook for audience building, fund raising, promotion, publicity and ticket sales — and for building general support for the arts as well as for the particular organization.

In training presenters, Affiliate Artists aims primarily at helping them to establish clear goals for the program. It is essential that every Informance they schedule underscore those goals. The goal may be as basic as introducing a performance discipline the community has had little exposure to. It may be as specific as meeting a fund-raising goal or increasing subscription sales.

Fort Wayne, Indiana is a typical example of how the program works. General Electric was the corporate sponsor for a full two-year program; the Fort Wayne Fine Arts Foundation, an umbrella organization that raises money for most of the major arts groups in town — the museum, dance company, symphony, theater companies, etc. — was the presenting organization. Through Affiliate Artists the foundation scheduled artists from varying disciplines to appear when its members were holding their respective subscription drives. Because Fort Wayne has no opera company, they scheduled two opera singers to stir an interest in that art form. To thank businesses that had contributed to their annual drive, they scheduled Affiliate Artists to perform in the workplace. Such performances have proved to be an effective way of building audiences directly and have given employees pride in what their companies are doing for the arts in the community.

Fort Wayne's six Affiliate Artists gave 118 Informances over a two-year period involving 12 weeks of residencies. Through Informances they reached 8,500 people, and more than 63 percent of these were adults who were potential audience members or contributors. In addition, 4,300 people attended the formal concerts that each artist gave at the end of the particular residency. Thus the live audience was 13,000; with press and media exposure, the program reached an additional 670,000. The artists made such an impression in Fort Wayne that the Fine Arts Foundation brought all six back to stage a gala event for the kick-off of their fund-raising campaign the next year. That event — a cabaret featuring solo and collaborative performances by the artists — was attended by 900 local business, community and cultural leaders. Not only were the Fort Wayne arts organizations pleased with the Affiliate Artists, but General Electric management saw that its support had been effectively and constructively used by the Fine Arts Foundation as presenter.

The Fort Wayne experience and its success in audience education and development are not unique: Affiliate Artists has evidence from many communities of the significant improvement it has brought about in public participation in the arts. Over time the programs have grown, both in number and variety. Society is wide open for much more of what Affiliate Artists has done. But there must be more and better efforts, because vast numbers of people are still not supporting the arts. Unfortunately, it seems unlikely that what performing and other arts institutions are doing will improve this very much. It is essentially a question of how to make the arts accessible to people. If all that is done is preaching to the already converted, to those already coming to performances, the chances of expanding the audience in number and sophistication are considerably diminished. It is imperative to go out into the community and the workplace and reach and teach people where they are.

# ARTS EDUCATION FOR
## special audiences

# ARTS EDUCATION FOR SPECIAL AUDIENCES

Corporations and community organizations are trying to bring the arts to publics who have not previously participated in them. Such efforts are invariably directed at able-bodied individuals, tending to neglect members of "special" or "unrealized" audiences, a total of approximately 60 to 90 million people for whom the arts and arts education programs are inaccessible because of a disability—a temporary or permanent impairment of hearing, sight or mobility.

Historically, arts organizations have been unresponsive to the needs of these special audiences. Yet at some point in life, everyone may experience such disabilities, if only because of aging. These populations are as interested and capable of learning as are those who are younger and more able-bodied. Indeed, in keeping with the purposes of a cultural democracy, the federal government in 1973 mandated that all publicly supported arts organizations provide accessibility for disabled persons. The National Endowment for the Arts has since implemented that mandate.

Paula Terry, of the Arts Endowment's Office for Special Constituencies, here discusses the size and special needs of these previously ignored audiences, citing examples of successful programs supported through the Endowment's Arts-in-Education Program.

Deborah Sonnenstrahl, a member of the faculty at Gallaudet University, describes her experience with the arts as a congenitally deaf child and her subsequent education in the arts at Gallaudet, the national university for the deaf. Her address, delivered by signing, was interpreted by Candy Broecker, an actress with the National Theater for the Deaf. Along with a reading by Ambrosia Shepherd, a published poet and honored teacher in a senior center in Washington, D.C., theirs were powerful performances.

These talks have generated new questions for a research agenda. Data from a national survey of what museums have done to increase accessibility, sponsored by the Smithsonian Institution, will help clarify whether and how programs for impaired and nonimpaired populations can be integrated.

The cost-effectiveness of specialized facilities, with their trained staffs, compared with programs fostering community access and education for non-handicapped populations, is still unknown. Program evaluation remains to be conducted, and standards against which to judge the quality of arts educational programs for adults must be developed. Access, however, remains the necessary first order of business — and it is more easily measured than the quality and success of the educational programs that will follow.

# THE ARTS ENDOWMENT'S PROGRAMS FOR SPECIAL CONSTITUENCIES

by Paula Terry

The National Endowment for the Arts has long been concerned about underserved populations and continues to work on all fronts to make the best cultural programs available to all citizens. Arts education serves this goal well, as artists produce and teach their art in a wide variety of settings outside the classroom. The National Council on the Arts resolved in 1973 that "arts are a right, not a privilege; and no citizen should be deprived of the beauty and insights into human experience that only the arts can impart."[1] Accordingly, through a variety of means—advocacy, technical assistance and funding—the Arts Endowment pursues the goal of ensuring that the arts are available and meaningful in the lives of people who represent special constituencies: older adults, people with various kinds of disabilities and those in institutions. This is not to keep such populations segregated, however. In the words of Arts Endowment Chairman Frank Hodsoll:

We clearly reject the notion that special or different arts programs should be developed for special constituencies and choose instead to find ways to open existing arts programs of the highest quality to these citizens. Special constituencies should become less special; we anticipate the time when it is commonplace to design environments and programs for all people.[2]

Across the country, people with various disabilities are exhibiting new interest in the arts, as arts and educational programs respond to the encouragement provided by the Endowment and other organizations for developing outreach to these large segments of the society. In August 1986, with support from the Endowment's Artists-in-Education Program, the University of California at Los Angeles sponsored a conference entitled Art

*Paula Terry is coordinator of the Office for Special Constituents of the National Endowment for the Arts.*

in Other Places, the first national conference in which educators, artists and administrators shared innovative teaching programs designed for alternative settings — from senior centers and nursing homes to correctional institutions.

A number of specific programs are worth mentioning. Creative Growth, in Oakland, California, provides visual arts classes for more than 100 mentally or emotionally disabled adults. The more talented students are paired one-to-one with professional artists, who work together and jointly exhibit their work. At present, four such students have paintings in the Oakland Museum rental gallery.

State and local arts agencies' Arts-in-Education grants have supported many professional artists who have worked with people in residential institutions. In Arkansas, visual artist Jorge Villegas works with resident students to create wall murals at centers for disabled persons. In Pueblo, Colorado, with funding from the Endowment's Inter-Arts Program, the Sangre de Cristo Arts and Conference Center has developed extensive educational programs with area nursing homes, retirement residences and health-care centers to cultivate general arts audiences among older people.

Lincoln Center for the Performing Arts in New York City is implementing an audience development project designed to increase the participation of disabled persons. Project director Ruth Knapp is surveying the Center's facilities and planning access improvements as well as collecting and assessing data on potential and previously neglected audiences.

Duke University Medical Center in Durham, North Carolina has established model programs of performing and visual arts for patients, staff and visitors. Included are a wide variety of classes, performances and exhibitions and a cultural resource information center. Along similar lines, the Arts Endowment has developed six pilot programs with the Veterans Administration (VA) to establish a series of arts residencies in VA hospitals. In one case, at the conclusion of a residency funded by the Arts Endowment, musician Kathy Wallenbarger was kept on as a full-time employee by the Mountain Home Veterans Medical Center in Johnson City, Tennessee. Specific profiles follow of the particular audiences such programs address.

## AUDIENCE PROFILES

**Older Adults.** It is well known that creative expression flourishes and matures during one's older years. The capacity to understand messages communicated in art seems to increase with age as experiences are expanded and perceptions are sharpened. Renowned anthropologist Margaret Mead has said: "It is utterly false and cruelly arbitrary to put all the learning into childhood, all the work into middle age, and all the regrets into old age."[3] The older segments of our population are rapidly growing, and this implies increased need in the arts. Americans 65 and older have outnumbered teenagers since mid-1983. Older people now number 28 million, whereas they numbered only three million at the turn of the century. In 1900, this figure represented four percent of the U.S. population; today, people 65 and older account for more than 12 percent. By the year 2000, people in this age group will represent 13 percent of a population better educated than ever before. Arts administrators and educators can anticipate greater participation in arts education programs from older people, as it is well known that a person's involvement in continuing education is directly linked to his or her formal education. In a new book entitled *Visual Arts and Older People,* artist/educator Dr. Pearl Greenberg points out:

More people than ever before can be expected to enjoy long lives and to continue to contribute to society. Never before have so many people remained in good health and lived long enough to be retired for so long. It has been estimated that by the year 2000 our average years of retirement might increase from 13 to 25 years. Getting people ready to use all of this additional lifetime requires educators well versed in a variety of different aspects of learning; the visual arts, music, dance, theater, prose and poetry can enhance our lives and involve older adults in stimulating and creative ways of living.[4]

The Arts Endowment's 1985 Survey of Public Participation in the Arts, which shows lower attendance rates for older people, provides a sharpened understanding of the relative importance of several barriers. Important differences show up in the perceived barriers to attendance by the older age groups, as compared with the population at large. For example, the population as a whole gave "not enough time" as the most frequently mentioned barrier, whereas the 65-and-over age group ranked this reason eighth. The complete analysis of these data shows a substantially different set of problems for older persons who want to participate compared with younger persons who want to participate. "Time" and "cost" drop in relative importance and, instead, factors of distance, travel, lack of companions and state of health become the critical barriers. The relative availability of leisure time and the reduced concern over expense indicate that older Americans are an audience ready to be tapped.

**Disabled People**. Disabled people are participating in a nationwide process aimed at achieving access to the arts. In 1973 Congress enacted legislation that would eventually benefit all disabled citizens. A provision of the Rehabilitation Act of 1973, Section 504 states:

No otherwise qualified handicapped individual in the United States shall, solely by reason of handicap, be excluded from the participation in, be denied the benefits of, or be subjected to discrimination under any program or activity receiving federal financial assistance.

In 1978, the Arts Endowment was the third federal agency to issue its 504 Regulation requiring recipients of federal funds to make their programs and services available to disabled people.

The U.S. Department of Health and Human Services estimates that disabled people constitute almost one-sixth of the population. Yet a person's needs and interest in the arts do not diminish because of temporary or permanent disability. For example:

- If the ability to hear should lessen, would one be forced to give up many arts activities? It is estimated that 4.4 million Americans are severely hearing-impaired. Today, many kinds of accommodations—such as audio amplification systems, subtitles and sign-language interpretation—enable individuals with this sensory impairment to fully appreciate art.

- Many of the more than ten million Americans who have visual impairments are experiencing performing arts activities by wearing small earphones through which they hear an audio description—live narration of movement, colors, scenery, etc. Large print materials and labeling as well as cassette recordings enable this population to perceive the written word.

- The inability to walk should not prevent anyone from participating in the arts. There are 11.7 million Americans who have impaired mobility and approximately 12.5 million whose mobility is temporarily impaired.

- The creative processes are equally important to the 6.8 million Americans experiencing mental or emotional disabilities.

**People Living in Institutions.** Is the best art available to citizens in institutions, such as hospitals, where more than one million Americans are at any given time? There are approximately one-half million people in state and federal correctional facilities. One and one-half million citizens are in convalescent and nursing care facilities, and almost two million are in other kinds of institutions. For those spending long periods of time in an institution, certainly the best arts programs are even more essential to improve the quality of life.

Because some people fall into more than one category, the exact figures for each group of older, disabled and institutionalized people are unknown. It is certain, however, that the number of special constituents is between 60 and 90 million Americans, and their number is increasing rapidly. The potential for growth in educational participation by these populations is enormous. Arts administrators and educators are being challenged to reassess who their priority audiences are.

## AUDIENCE DEVELOPMENT

Access to the arts is creating new and larger audiences for arts education programs. Audience development efforts have grown out of this newly created awareness. An important consideration in opening up arts education programs to people who fall into these categories is, first and foremost, that they are people. False images and stereotypes of older and disabled persons have led to social policies and programs that tend to perpetuate negative images. Public policy makers, for example, frequently assume that older adults and people with disabilities need to be "taken care of" when, in fact, the same principle of education for independence and for contributions to society should be considered for older and disabled people as for younger and "able" people. More and more organizations are becoming aware of the architectural, programmatic, financial and attitudinal barriers to people's participation in arts and education programs.

Staff training is an essential component in developing these unrealized audiences for arts education programs. The National Trust for Historical Preservation assumed a leadership role by providing its membership with a series of six regional workshops to address the architectural and programmatic needs of older and disabled visitors. Site directors worked with an advisory committee, composed of older adults and disabled persons, who discussed constraints posed by historic properties and assisted in evaluating current programs. The two-day workshops, hosted at historic sites in six states, were attended by 107 site managers and other staff representing more than 300 historic sites from 14 states. As a result, the participating sites have undertaken many accommodations to make the properties more accessible to everyone. Due to the remarkable success of this effort, the National Trust plans to conduct additional workshops in California, Missouri, New York and Texas.

Training programs of this type should include information on how language can increase attitudinal barriers. Labeling a person by a disability or by age is inappropriate. For example, what kinds of people are visualized when someone says "the aged," "the elderly" or "the handicapped"? Imagine that everyone in the society weighs a maximum of 100 pounds — except you and two million other Americans. Therefore, the built environment, including chairs, the subway system, restaurants and

An excerpt from the poem, *Rev. Jesse Jackson, 1984*
by Ambrosia Shepherd

Jesse said, "We must move again."
And we must move again.
We must move beyond the steady diet
Of              I'm sick,
                      I'm sad,
                and I'm poor.
Because,           I ain't sick,
                   I ain't sad,
                and I ain't poor.
And            I ain't marketing no blues,
        I ain't marketing nothing I can't use.
I ain't marketing no blues,
I ain't marketing nothing but good news.

I ain't marketing no blues,
Because you'll become what
                you say you are,
                as a man thinketh
                in his heart
                so is he.
So      I ain't marketing no blues,
    I ain't marketing nothing but good news.
Leaving all negative thoughts behind us,
Dealing with truth to the death,
Dealing with truth to the death,
The truth to the death.
                Amen.

Ambrosia Shepherd is a poet, a literary panelist for the Arts and Humanities
Commission, Washington, D.C. and a teacher in Arts Mentor Program for
The National Council on Aging.

restrooms, is designed primarily for 100-pound people. However, accommodations are available for larger people. Program materials might read
"Accommodations for the Fat" and state that "fat seating is available in the
front and back rows of this auditorium," or "fat stalls are available in the
restroom," or "there is a fat phone booth just outside the meeting room."
More appropriate would be "Accommodations for Larger People," in the

same way that "Accommodations for Disabled People" is more appropriate.

Another example of a successful arts education program, supported through the Arts Endowment's Artists-in-Education Program, is the Arts Mentor Program. Developed by Priscilla McCutcheon, past director of the Center on Arts and Aging of the National Council on Aging (NCOA), this model effort has trained older professional artists to teach in schools and senior centers. Following an intensive training session, 12 artists were placed in such sites, where they taught for eight weeks – and seven of them are still there. One of these is poet Ambrosia Shepherd, a recipient of grants from Poets and Writers and a literary panelist for the Arts and Humanities Commission in Washington, D.C. Her senior center students have videotaped a collective presentation of their own poetry.

Her program and the entire project are documented in *The Arts Mentor Program,* a book available from NCOA describing step-by-step how to develop such a program. Also available is *The Arts and 504 Handbook,* which the Arts Endowment produced to help arts organizations make their activities more accessible to people with disabilities. It contains a section on staff training as well as audience development and is available free from state arts councils or by purchase from the Government Printing Office.

All of the programs described here – except Creative Growth – have resulted from cooperative efforts between a variety of institutions and the Office for Special Constituencies at the Arts Endowment. New project proposals and initiatives that will increase access and education in the arts across the country are always welcomed.

## NOTES

1. From a resolution approved by the National Council for the Arts at their 32nd meeting, in September 1973.
2. Speech by Frank M. Hodsoll on July 14, 1983, at the National Symposium on Access to Cultural Programs, Bloomington, Indiana.
3. Margaret Mead, *I Hope They Keep Coming* (Iowa Arts Council, 1976).
4. Pearl Greenberg, *Visual Arts and Older People* (Springfield, Ill.: Charles C. Thomas, 1987).

# ARTS EDUCATION FOR DEAF POPULATIONS

## by Deborah Sonnenstrahl

Even though I was born deaf I was taken to art museums and theaters as a child. This was during the Dark Ages, before the Rehabilitation Act had been passed. There were no interpreting services for deaf visitors and accessibility was at its barest minimum. Nonetheless, my parents never gave up hope that they had instilled in me a love of the arts and theater. At the time, their ventures met with little success. I could not hear the words spoken on the stage or by a museum docent, but being an obedient child, I trailed after my mother, aimlessly killing time by looking at pictures or at actors while my mother listened to the words and tried to enunciate them to me. Almost all of their content was lost on me, however. I could not look at the art and at my mother's face or hands at the same time.

By the age of 12, I rebelled: no more museums or theater for me. My parents, though disappointed, were powerless to resolve the problem. My resistance crumbled during my sophomore year at Gallaudet University, when I was required to take a course in art history. I finally understood what art was all about. Deaf people are visually oriented, as everything they learn or know has to pass through their eyes. Therefore, art history is considered one of the most valuable courses in Gallaudet's curriculum.

## GALLAUDET UNIVERSITY

Gallaudet University, in Washington D.C., has been the world's only liberal arts college for deaf students since its establishment in 1864. In the last 10 years, the university has expanded its already strong commitment to the arts, particularly to the educational aspects of the arts and artwork of museum quality. It has developed a program linking the university to

*Deborah Sonnenstrahl is associate professor of art history and museum studies at Gallaudet University.*

museums across the country; it has mounted an elderhostel program along with continuing education programs; and it has set up a Fine Arts in Education Office, funded by the National Endowment for the Arts and the National Endowment for the Humanities.

Not all deaf or hearing-impaired people are going to Gallaudet University or to any college of higher education. However, my personal experience may help suggest how any deaf individual's special needs can be met. There are now many programs across the nation for deaf people. New York University is a good example. Because New York University maintains a student special services office I was able to engage interpreting services without going through the exhausting logistics of finding an interpreter. I am currently a doctoral student in combined fields of Museum Studies and Deaf Education and was promoted to the rank of Associate Professor of Art History and Museum Studies last year. [*Editor's Note:* The author received her doctoral degree in May 1987.] Because of the excellent Museum Studies program at New York University I was able to implement a new major, Museum Studies, in the Gallaudet University Art Department curriculum last year. I also interned at the Museum of Modern Art in New York City for four months to meet some of New York University's requirements. I selected the Museum of Modern Art as my internship site because it has been one of New York's most accessible museums and one offering interpreted tours; therefore, deafness was not unfamiliar to the museum professionals. I believe I am the first deaf person to hold a professional Museum certificate. And this is only the beginning for both deaf museum professionals and visitors.

Gallaudet University has succeeded in making arts education available in four ways to deaf people who are not enrolled in the University.

**Liaison Between Gallaudet University and Museums.** Gallaudet has long recognized the need to make programs accessible for deaf people, particularly in arts education outside the classroom. Through the art department a new major, Museum Studies, was included in the curriculum in 1985. A faculty member of the Museum Studies program has been involved in museum planning committees and several advisory boards. Therefore, Gallaudet is linked to museums and encourages them to invite hearing-impaired individuals to serve on these committees of advisory boards. Those individuals have contacts with outside audiences which can become a drawing card for the museum. Though the Museum Studies program is new, having only one faculty member in the department, the benefits are already apparent. This faculty member has been asked by organizations representing deaf people to present "pep talks" to their constituents on how to enjoy a museum visit.

Interpreters are the link between deaf and hearing individuals. However, because the deaf individual is visually oriented, using an interpreter lessens impact. He or she needs to absorb all the facts available, whether through expressions on the speaker's face or a wave or flourish of a certain hand sign to convey a message. The University has learned that to reach the deaf audience, the docent has to be compatible with their mode of education and communication. Students in the Museum Studies program should be hired as docents as they "speak" the audience's language, which would make deaf visitors' trips more stimulating and pleasant.

Three Gallaudet students are currently working on their internships in three museums: Gallaudet Museum, the National Archives, and the National Museum of American Art, all in Washington, D.C. The Capitol Children's Museum has employed a deaf museum professional for the past two years. Both the Capitol Museum and the National Park Service use deaf persons as docents, and each attracts a large audience of deaf visitors.

**Elderhostel.** Gallaudet University's National Academy presents an Elderhostel Week every summer, which has proved to be the most successful program in arts education beyond the classroom. Designed for older deaf persons, the program was a catalyst in developing art awareness for special audiences. In summer 1986, 50 deaf persons from all over the nation participated in the program, which offered two courses, "Why Art History" and "How to Enjoy an Art Museum." They learned about art styles that have evolved through the history of mankind and about influences that have shaped artistic efforts. The most important result of the program was motivating these people to visit museums as part of their humanistic education. Participants have written to say they are continuing to visit museums in their home towns.

The program evaluations were so positive that the administration has increased the courses from three days to a full week. These deaf people were retired and hence had considerable leisure time. Therefore they needed to know how to get maximum benefit from their art museum visits. In addition, they learned how to ask for reasonable auxiliary services which kept the museums' costs to a minimum. The National Academy has received requests for other such programs in cities which have heavy concentrations of older persons who are, as they put it, "tired of playing cards all day." Because hearing loss is common among the elderly, this population should receive a high priority.

**Continuing Education.** Gallaudet University also maintains Continuing Education programs geared toward hearing-impaired adults. Classes in ceramics, art history, sculpture and watercolor have been offered.

**Fine Arts in Education.** Though now defunct, the Fine Arts in Education Office was Gallaudet's most ambitious project in arts education beyond the classroom. Through three years (1980-1983) of support from the National Endowment for the Humanities and the National Endowment for the Arts, the project was able to reach deaf audiences on the widest possible scale. To meet the requirement for a visually-oriented environment on the University campus, the administration adopted a policy for establishing a museum without walls. Exhibitions were not confined, as they are at most colleges and universities, to a single designated university gallery. Artwork was and still is displayed all over the campus and in buildings elsewhere at one time or another. The entire University complex was essentially treated as a museum, but one without walls, serving the entire community. For instance, Lloyd Hamrol's *Stonewall* was in front of the University Center, a Rodin sculpture (on loan) once graced the Field House lobby, and a Matisse was in the Model Secondary School for the Deaf. These exhibitions gave both young and older deaf people opportunities to become familiar with the works of major artists.

Because of the importance of such exposure, the University's Art Department has undertaken the functions and responsibilities of the Fine Arts in Education Office, though on a smaller scale due to limited faculty resources.

## IMMEDIATE AND LONG-RANGE CHALLENGES

Attracting, educating and maintaining hearing-impaired people's interest and motivation to continue their arts education has proved challenging. Deaf museum professionals emphasize that it is essential to work with deaf people in devising effective accommodations and reaching this audience. To ensure compliance with Section 504 of the Rehabilitation Act, hearing-impaired members of advisory committees can make valuable contributions to discussions of policy changes needed to improve access for disabled visitors in general. However, to assist efficiently with specific accommodations for the deaf, they should meet separately with staff members who are directly concerned with the problem so they can communicate without distraction. Docents will learn much from meeting with articulate deaf persons if a professional interpreter is present to expedite communication.

To reach deaf audiences, it is important to develop contact with leaders of clubs, centers and other community organizations for deaf people. If a museum staff member presents an introductory slide show at a center for deaf people, center personnel can interpret it and help members arrange visits to the museum. Deaf docents can also publicize the museum's accessibility through an efficient network of personal contacts. The museum may also wish to focus on the vigorous and articulate culture of the deaf in a special exhibit of deaf artists whose works are exhibited in museums, possibly for Deaf Awareness Week.

It is also important to continue publicity in all visual media that reach deaf people and their hearing friends, including the museum's regular brochures and news releases. Members of centers for deaf people can be reached through posters on their bulletin boards, items in their newsletters and mailings about special events. Captioning television programs and movies and interpreting at public events other than arts education programs are other important methods. Nothing needs to be costly or elaborate. Deaf people watch television a great deal, and if all art programs were captioned, they could inspire deaf people to go to museums to see the real thing. Large museums that already have television commercials can have 60-second announcements captioned for the closed-circuit network for $155 by the National Captioning Institute.

In conclusion, what has worked for me as a deaf person would work for any deaf person had he or she the opportunity. And what works for a deaf person would work for anybody with normal hearing. The following example illustrates this: I was viewing a Treasure of British Homes exhibition at the National Gallery of Art last year and was fortunate to get hold of a written script to compensate for the audio-tour. I accidentally bumped into a hearing friend who blurted out, "You are lucky!" It appeared he was stuck with the speed of the recording; if he lost his place he had to rewind and rewind until he found his place again. I had no such problem. Had all these aids been available during the so-called Dark Ages of Deafness, my parents would not have been so frustrated and I would not have experienced such growing pains.

# ARTS EDUCATION IN

## museums

# ADULT ARTS EDUCATION IN MUSEUMS

The preservation and presentation of great art constitute the primary purpose of art museums. Thus museums can respond to Samuel Lipman's challenge to focus their educational programs on great artworks. Yet they must also respond to the demands of a cultural democracy for the inclusion of diverse artworks and expanded audiences. Museums face the dilemma of upholding established aesthetic standards while trying to reach previously neglected populations through works new audiences may find more accessible and interesting. Museum personnel ask whether they can — and should — tailor their programs to suit all possible audiences. Even if those questions are answered affirmatively, much remains unknown about the demographics and tastes of various groups; more information is needed so that successful educational programs can be designed.

Such issues reflect conflicting priorities within the museum hierarchy. Museum education departments remain stepchildren of curatorial departments, which focus on the collection, preservation and promotion of unique art objects. Likewise, new technologies present additional opportunities and problems for museum educators. Capable of reaching vast new audiences, those technologies are costly and compete with traditional museum education programs as well as curatorial commitments.

Each museum's educational mission reflects its collection and audiences. Philip Yenawine, director of education for the Museum of Modern Art, is concerned with the evident difficulty that even highly educated audiences have in understanding contemporary art. At the Metropolitan Museum of Art, educators must deal with an encyclopedic museum and more diverse audiences. Katherine Lochridge, former director of community education, takes the position that responsible museum education programs must be physically, economically, socially and psychologically accessible to all persons. She faces many problems. What mix of entertainment and education is best in a program? Are collaborative efforts with outside agencies either possible or desirable? As a response to such questions, the Metropolitan Museum is restructuring its entire Division of Educational Services.

These issues, which have concerned museum educators for some time, are also of increasing importance to other arts organizations — symphony orchestras, theaters, dance companies — which traditionally have been less concerned about audience education, particularly adult education. These organizations can no longer avoid educational efforts, as their current audience is growing older, and younger populations appear to be less informed and to attend less often. Museums thus present a model in their attempts to balance art presentation and art education.

# MUSEUM ARTS EDUCATION IN VISUAL LITERACY

**by Philip Yenawine**

For many people, contemporary art is difficult to understand without help, but art in general, no matter how minor or great, whether folk art or fine art, is not enough a part of the fabric of most people's lives to be adequately appreciated without some assistance. Certainly there are artworks that everyone can understand—beautiful landscape paintings or photographs. Even for these works, however, aesthetic experience is enhanced by knowing where the work comes from, how old it is, what technique was used in making it, what the original subject was, etc. Without such information, the experience of the work is seldom rich enough to be called "educational."

Samuel Lipman has raised the issue of the "miracle" of great art. It is unlikely that an uninitiated viewer can approach, for instance, Agnes Martin's minimally marked, mostly white canvases, Jackson Pollock's challenges to conventional aesthetics, or most contemporary art for that matter, expecting to get caught up in some miracle. Both knowledge and experience are required before that level of communication occurs. A broad conception of the artistic experience should not require it to be some kind of miracle or mystery. The "miracle" of great art is probably no more teachable than spirituality is. Such experience is probably innate. Even if the mystery of art is teachable, it is unlikely that it could be presented to people in the framework of adult education. Rather, as Mr. Lipman emphasized in his insistence on a basic knowledge of artistic practice, what is required is more fundamental and perhaps more important. The meaningful experience of art inevitably requires learning something new. Learning must start from the ground up.

Something most interesting about the art of our own time can, however, be taught and learned. That is the way it subverts the expected—whether

*Philip Yenawine is director of education at the Museum of Modern Art.*

beauty or magic or simply recognizable subject matter. On many levels most contemporary art assails the assumptions that people bring to art. And because of this subversion, art gives people opportunities to exercise their perceptions, their emotional responses and their intellects in equal measure. A painting by Robert Rauschenberg can open people's minds because to understand it involves an important thinking process. As educators, those in museums are responsible for providing the few essential words that will give people enough comfort with what is in front of them so that they can take the next steps themselves. Such comfort usually comes through information—sometimes through discussing the artists' intentions, sometimes pointing out what the titles might mean, most often analyzing the subject, style and content. All of this helps people to identify and in turn to understand what they are actually looking at.

The results of recent audience surveys conducted at the Museum of Modern Art show how necessary such educational efforts are. The Museum has an "upscale" and educated audience. The median income of its visitors (similar to that found by the American Museum of Natural History among the readership of its magazine) is just under $50,000 a year; 70 percent have gone to college; 40 percent have gone to graduate school; and 70 percent of those with college educations have studied some art history. Most visitors are over age 40 and thus attended college before modern art became a standard part of art history curricula, so however well educated they may be, most lack academic preparation for twentieth-century art. The further paradox is that the study of art history has made some people more humble in the presence of contemporary artworks, because they appreciate how much richer their experience could become if they knew more about the art in front of them.

Not surprisingly, 90 percent of the Museum's visitors expect to find instructional material available should they want it, which 60 percent of them say they do. They also have strong feelings about the forms such help should take. The preferred device is wall labels, probably because they are short, accessible and usually easy to read. The physical placement next to the work may be central to the popularity of labels. Other printed materials, such as brochures, can embody all of the above virtues and also be taken away with the viewer. Another model information device that should be explored further is handouts, such as those the National Gallery of Art makes available in each gallery, concerning individual works and groupings of works. One advantage of such handouts is that people can sit and rest while they read them. Moreover, handouts do not create congestion as labels often do. (Of course, there is then the need for benches in the galleries for visitors to sit on while reading.) As for recorded tours, or "acoustiguides," most people dislike them. In the survey, 12 percent found them only distracting, and the same proportion, 12 percent, like to use them. Some people are unenthusiastic about group lectures because they interrupt other people's concentration, but lectures are not disliked as much as recorded guides, which inevitably deny people's sense of autonomy and control over their own direction.

In any event, The Museum of Modern Art's visitors disagree with the standard museum argument that art "speaks for itself." Modern and contemporary art functions heavily on conceptual levels, reverberating very much in the heads of the artists before it is even produced. As a result, its intellectual content may be unapproachable from the standpoint of what one can actually see. This is also true of historical art, but people think that they understand older art because they can recognize its subject matter. Still, if they do not know the mythology or who is depicted or the iconography, they are unlikely to get the message in the way it was intended, and they certainly will not get the same message that was conveyed to the person who saw it in its original context.

So even with historical art, people have to make leaps. Each time they do, when something is not immediately accessible as it is on television or in advertising, background and even "foreground" information is of crucial assistance to us. But before people are willing to make leaps, from an entry level, they need to know what they know. Until they do, they are unprepared for anything open-ended. Thus to prepare people for the unknown, museum staffs have to tell them some things, explain others (such as the formal elements of a painting's structure), engage them with illustrations and comparisons and affect their curiosity, helping them become aware of what the museum and they have done, in terms of process and results. So ultimately the experience of a Rauschenberg is going to be one in which they are comfortable with its being a heap of images adding up to something different for every person, perhaps differently every time.

Learning to be comfortable with such openness is not inherently difficult, and it can certainly happen in the time people allow for adult education programs, including museum visits. This does not necessarily mean that the museum actually teaches it now, or that it has the trained, knowledgeable staff and techniques on hand. But it is possible to do if the attainment of such visual literacy—for that is what it is—is finally defined as the goal. Empowering people to see for themselves does not require that they agree with a museum's interpretation. More power is given (or taken) when they do not. It is therefore most important to teach an approach to unfamiliar material, to encourage open dialogue and debate, and to view the job as providing keys that people themselves can place in the locks of the doors they want to open.

This discussion of museums has focused on them as places for the general public rather than as places that produce catalogs or that attract scholars to look at definitive collections and exhibitions. The reason those functions are not covered here is that, basically, most museums perform them very well. What museums must now begin to address are the broader needs of the large spectrum of people who constitute their current audiences — to say nothing of those who are too intimidated or simply too disinterested to join them. By supplying "entry level" information rather than definitive statements, museums will make it possible for more people to take the next steps on their own, as increasingly visually literate adults.

# MUSEUM ACCESS: PLANNING FOR DIVERSE AUDIENCES

## by Katherine Lochridge

Increasingly, people are selecting museums for some of their educational or entertainment needs, and these visitors are broadly representative of the variety present in a pluralistic society. The escalating costs of museum programming, coupled with shrinking dollar support and the reliance of most museums on tax-based philanthropy, make it imperative that museums increase their efforts to plan programs reflective of this diversity in museum audiences. Museum administrators need to be attuned to what these visitors may need — what types of programs, on what subjects, in what languages, etc. — to plan for increased use of the museum as a learning tool or educational resource.

Although museums cannot guarantee that learning will take place or that the learning environment will be universally successful, certainly they can aim at providing economic access (with reasonable admission and subscription fees) and physical access (with special services for the elderly and the disabled, for example) as minimum goals. Social or psychological access is a more difficult issue. Every museum visitor has his or her own individual experience and personal history. In designing museum experiences for a particular audience, planners must immediately address the question of whether programming should be tailored for a specific constituency, "mainstreamed" within the programming for general populations, or both. In most large museums, there is a duality about programs for special constituencies in that efforts are made to tailor some programs to the needs of the particular sociological group while also ensuring the group's access to every aspect of general programming. An acknowledgment of cultural differences, of the different ways of "seeing," of the choices of what objects to

---

*Katherine Lochridge is the former director of community education at the Metropolitan Museum of Art.*

look at and even the methods of presentation may be necessary to ensure educational success for a particular audience.

At the Metropolitan Museum of Art these issues have been the subject of lengthy discussions internally and among community advisors. Does the Rockefeller Wing's emphasis on primitive art and the arts of Africa and Oceania appeal to black and Hispanic audiences, or does French Impressionism (a popular favorite with traditional museum audiences) appeal more? And are museum personnel presumptuous in either direction when they suggest that they know which appeals more and why? In the Metropolitan's nomenclature, "community audiences" has meant "special constituencies" or groups who are underserved or who have not been primary users in the past. This has been true since 1970, when the Department of Community Education was formed to serve as a programming area and a museumwide liaison for members of the Hispanic and bilingual community, the black community, the elderly and disabled visitors. The organizational structure of the entire Division of Education Services at the Museum dates from the same period, and the structure reflects sociopolitical concerns of the times. The Division was organized by audiences. Departments were vertically integrated, providing all programs and services for their particular audience, with little overlap or collaboration among them. Such a structure had a specific rationale. Specialists in working with particular audiences were grouped together, tailoring programs for those specific audiences.

A Long Range Planning Study, completed in 1986, suggests an alternative organizational model. After exhaustive group interviews and surveys with members of various audience segments, it was determined that, although services could continue to be specialized or tailored for specific audiences, the organizational structure should be more lateral to permit the sharing of resources among departments and to provide more general mainstream program alternatives for the public.

A high-school audience, for example, is similar to an audience of adults who are novice museum visitors. The question can then be formulated as, "Can one design appropriate programs that will be interesting and informative for adults and young people simultaneously?" or "Should all programs be designed without regard to ethnicity, language spoken or specific requirements of a particular audience?" The answers to those questions are probably yes, no and both. Most concede that, to attract diverse and new audiences, both mainstream and specialized programs should be offered.

Another aspect of planning for diverse audiences is that, before designing new initiatives to attract such audiences, museums should look at those audiences systematically. Taking a lesson from market research, museums need research on various populations – full demographic characteristics, education levels (a leading indicator of participation in cultural programs) and interests. In the Metropolitan's case, such continued study has fostered a program design better meeting the cultural and educational needs of the various groups. Obviously, that is not the same thing as asking people what they like and giving it to them through programs. In a recent survey of 4,000 teachers in the metropolitan area, the Metropolitan found that the preferred format was the one-day curriculum-related workshop offered in the summer months. Some highly successful pilot programs were developed based on that design information.

Ultimately, the goal is to provide for the objects in the collections a context that will resonate within the cultural contexts from which the audiences come. An object's time period, maker, iconography and formal attributes should be related to the cultural reality or experiences of diverse audiences. The Metropolitan, with its encyclopedic collections, is in a position to do that better than most museums. Staff have given, and will continue to give, much attention to the development of programs and materials that stress the "connectedness" of various cultures and time periods. For example, discussions have begun with LaGuardia Community College in western Queens about the role the Museum's diverse collections could play in enriching the education of a LaGuardia-sponsored multicultural high school populated entirely by young people from other countries.

It will be necessary to structure partnerships to deliver services and programs to diverse audiences. Community agencies or schools might be unfamiliar with the resources an art museum could provide. Conversely, museums are generally less a part of the intimate community network than are certain churches and social service agencies. In a city the size of New York, with the Metropolitan Museum (and most museums) organized around the principle of informal or "casual" learning, viable partnerships can ensure greater museum access to nontraditional groups.

In summary, assuring diverse audience groups of access to the nation's museum-held treasures requires commitment and planning. An organizational structure that permits lateral communication and cooperation along with systematic study of audiences can yield valuable information for sensitive program design. Within that framework, skilled museum teachers using contextual approaches can work with cooperative partners to further these objectives. However, the actual success rate cannot be measured, because the ultimate achievement is that of the new, lifelong museum-goers who had not felt a part of it before.

# ARTS EDUCATION AND
## the mass media

# ARTS EDUCATION AND THE MASS MEDIA

In most arts organizations, any media-based arts education programming competes with the production, preservation and performance of the arts themselves. On television, arts programming competes with other television offerings — for audiences and for funding. From the point of view of arts organizations, the arts come before arts education *regardless* of audience; from the point of view of television, even educational television, entertainment comes before both the arts and the education, *because* of the audience. Thomas Newman of the Metropolitan Museum of Art and Robert Kotlowitz, vice president for the arts and humanities for WNET/Channel 13, raise questions about the possible success of television broadcasting of the visual arts, as opposed to the performing arts. Despite obstacles, both agree that the mass media can provide access to the arts and to great artworks among vast audiences who would otherwise never experience them "live."

Thomas Newman points out that film and television have filled ancillary roles in museum education programs for some time.[1] The question remains about whether they inevitably falsify and in time may replace the direct aesthetic experience of viewing original work. Yet Arts Endowment surveys of arts audiences demonstrate that television and other broadcast media complement active arts participation, rather than serving as a direct substitute for it. Despite the liabilities of second-hand viewing and their very real expense, new media technologies offer many opportunities for arts educators. With these technologies, educators can both reach new audiences and bring them across the first threshold of aesthetic awareness into full participation as well as develop the sequential arts educational curriculum advocated by Samuel Lipman. The innovative use of museum-produced media packages could be vital to the success of collaborative efforts between museums and other arts organizations, such as community agencies, corporations, elderhostels and residences for disabled persons.

Robert Kotlowitz recognizes that exposure to, and familiarity with, the arts is the necessary first step to bringing adults with relatively little previous exposure into direct contact with the arts. Toward this end, he suggests innovative visual arts scheduling. He also suggests an increased use of video cassettes, produced in collaboration with established arts and educational institutions, artists and educators. The first step is to make the commitment to go beyond the status quo.

# NEW COMMUNICATION TECHNOLOGIES

by Thomas Newman

Along with increases in the size and diversity of museum audiences in the last decade, there has been a proliferation of new communication technologies. Together, these have added new fuel to the long-standing controversy about using such media for museum education.

To be sure, the use of television to reach the mass public is not new. The Metropolitan Museum of Art began television broadcasting in 1941, when most TV sets were in bars and hotel lobbies (a directory of places to watch TV was available from the Museum information desk).[1] Art museums in Boston and St. Louis, among other cities, participated in the founding of local educational television stations a few years later.

Since then, there has been no argument that television helps museums to reach a wider audience. The concern has arisen, however, that electronically transmitted knowledge of visual art is at best only a limited version — and at worst a complete distortion of the "live" aesthetic experience. There is something unique about the museum experience of original works of art which no transmission can capture. Most curators, and to a lesser degree most museum educators, believe that this direct, ineffable and nonintellectual experience can be diluted by too much information. Accordingly, the original function, context and current commodity value of an artwork are regarded as largely irrelevant to its appreciation for its own sake. From this perspective, it can be argued that museums do everyone a disservice by attempting to serve an untutored mass audience who focus on such irrelevancies at the expense of a pure aesthetic experience. Indeed, to discourage such nonaesthetic responses, informative labels should be almost eliminated: time spent reading would be better spent in looking.[2]

Yet the purist museum curators are unlikely to try to stimulate greater

---

*Thomas Newman is media specialist at the Metropolitan Museum of Art.*

direct visual attention by the method that is used – if for other reasons – in many Italian churches. These are usually dimly lit, and the visitor must deposit coins to turn on the lights for a minute or so to see the altarpieces. Few can take their eyes off the pictures until the timer runs out. But therefore they cannot simultaneously be reading background information from guidebooks. The effects are the same in museum exhibitions with few labels: however much the visual attention is enhanced, an opportunity to communicate with the unknowledgeable viewer is lost.

The museum philosophy of placing priority on aesthetics contrasts with the way in which television producers present visual art. Such programs are traditionally all context, all history and process, hardly focusing on the art itself.

Rarely has television shown visual art the way it shows the performing arts. Imagine watching a television production of the opera *Il Trovatore* that was shot the way most visual arts programming is done. After a few bars of the "Anvil Chorus," the host would step into the picture, talking over the music, giving his thoughts about the symbolism of the anvil and the life Verdi was leading when he composed the opera. Then the camera would return to the opera for a few seconds for a transition to a scene of a blacksmith's shop and a discussion of iron working and the late Industrial Revolution. The actual work of art, the opera, would be glimpsed, but no sustained attention would be paid to it as an aesthetic whole. Such an approach to televising visual art, although not the performing arts, is a convention of broadcasting, not a constraint of the technology itself.

Some would say that the current state of production is the result of audience demand, that documentaries follow a style calculated to hold the attention of as large an audience as possible. Even so, the audience for cultural programs remains small. One recent study found that only 4 percent of the TV households in the United States watch as much as three and three-quarter hours a month of cultural programming on public television.[3] This contradicts older surveys which indicated broad demand for cultural fare on TV.[4] In light of these findings, the failure of "narrowcasting" cable TV, promised in the early 1980s as a palliative to lowest-common-denominator commercial programming, is understandable. Broadcast television, even in conjunction with cable services, is not the answer to the art museum's need to reach new audiences. Perhaps, as has been said, educational television is a contradiction in terms.

## USES OF NEW MEDIA

More innovative approaches will be needed if museums are to avoid the same pitfalls with the new communications technologies. No one has yet found a strategy that works consistently and on a large scale, but some features typifying successful use of the new media for museum-based arts education can be described.

**New Instructional Tools.** The technologies themselves are in a period of rapid evolution, with breakthroughs to be regularly expected. The trends are fairly evident, however. The new technologies store information at a declining cost, and in ever-smaller containers. They allow access to that information, and perform linked computer-based functions faster than before. They combine with each other, producing hybrids. An illustration is the compact audio disc, which, following the home video boom, has stimulated renewed interest in the videodisc. The videodisc, in various, almost indestructible formats, can contain huge amounts of information (audio, video, numerical). It will become widely used by museum registrars and catalogers to keep track of museum collections. At the same time, that information can be retrieved so quickly that it supports individualized interactive programming. Thus the videodisc holds rich potential as an instructional tool, as a visual data base or in a synthesis now unimagined.

**Expansion of Museum Publishing.** The technology now being developed will lead to the expansion of museum publishing. Until now, museums were greatly concerned about the relatively poor visual quality of the image in electronic media. Now, however, new "high-definition" television is providing pictures of astonishing brilliance, and such television will eventually be available in our homes. Not coincidentally, book illustrations can be printed from electronic storage devices stemming from the same technology as high-definition television, and in some cases book content, including illustrations, may be available either in hard copy or electronically. This suggests that the publishing industry and the electronic media may be integrated. There is evidence that this is already happening: whereas at the 1984 American Booksellers Convention, only one publisher exhibited video, in 1986, 70 book publishers did so.[5] Art book publishing, with its heavy reliance on high-quality images, may lead in developing booklike visual data bases. Museums will be the source of the illustrations and background information of educational potential.

**Enlarged Revenue Sources.** New technologies will provide expanded sources of revenue for museums, partially offsetting their costs. Some studies suggest that the new media will cause people to spend more leisure time at home instead of in public places like museums. However, there are contrary indications that people are likely to spend increased leisure time going out to seek social experiences[6] Art museums will benefit from wider use of the media, as the performing arts already have, because watching programs about visual art will stimulate desire to see the originals. The stimulus provided by television for attendance at live dance performances is an example. Following the first broadcasts of "Dance in America," ticket sales to dance performances rose from 1 million to 16 million. Over the same period, museum admissions, not stimulated by any significant media outreach, barely doubled.[7] With greater and more sophisticated media coverage augmenting existing museum programs, an enriched under-standing of visual art will in turn lead to additional sources of revenue to museums through increased admissions and memberships as well as through direct sales of video cassettes.

**Greater Audience Research.** The increasing need for multiple sources of income and the related need for public accountability, resulting from greater government funding, will increase the pressure on museums to gather more reliable information about their audiences. Until now, large en-dowments have tended to insulate museums from the marketplace and the need to compete for audiences.[8] Accordingly, museums have not had to pay attention to visitors' needs for information of various kinds. The desultory use of mass media has been consistent with this neglect, but new tech-nologies allowing communication and education for smaller and more spe-cialized audience segments will require that museums pay more attention to audience needs. Successful museum education programs will increasingly be guided by audience research.

## CONCLUSION

It may seem that the new technologies have a life of their own. Yet these inventions came about because they were needed. Museums, too, need them, and need them greatly if they are to keep up with the increasing demands for information being made by new audiences. If the museum is to continue to fulfill its mission as a communicator of culture, it must develop the mechanisms, both organizational and technological, to adapt to social change.

## NOTES

1. "The Museum's Television Program," *Bulletin of the Metropolitan Museum of Art,* July 1941.

2. Sherman Lee, "The Museum as a Wilderness Area," *Museum News,* October 1972.

3. David Waterman, "The Failure of Cultural Programming on Cable TV: an Economic Interpretation," *Journal of Communication,* Summer 1986.

4. Ronald E. Frank and Marshall G. Greenberg, *Audiences for Public Television* (Beverly Hills: Sage, 1982).

5. Richard Zacks, "Cassettes Rewrite Studio's Books," *Channels Field Guide,* 1987.

6. Jonathan Gershuny, "Time Use Trends and Technological Innovation: a Seven Nation Comparison," presented at the Annual Conference of the American Association for Public Opinion Research (Hershey, Pa: 1987).

7. National Endowment for the Arts, "Arts and Cultural Programs on Television" (Washington, D.C.: 1977).

8. Paul DiMaggio, "The Nonprofit Instrument and the Influence of the Marketplace on Policies in the Arts," in *The Arts and Public Policy in the United States,* edited by W. McNeil Lowry (Englewood Cliffs, N.J.: Prentice-Hall, 1984).

# THE ARTS IN THE MASS MEDIA

## by Robert Kotlowitz

Making television programs about the visual arts is a difficult business. If fear and trembling have paralyzed producers and commercial sponsors over the years, who is to say that all have been cowards, given the cost of television production and the competition of rival channels, let alone of live arts events? The questions producers face are numerous and the answers are unclear. How can one make television programs about the arts that will educate as well as entertain? How does one stay faithful to the spirit of a work without creating a cloud of smothering reverence and losing the audience? How can one dramatize, without inflating, the roles of great cultural institutions in American life? Is an immobile object, frozen in time and space, distorted if, to capture its aesthetic and spiritual dynamism, it is made to seem to move on the television screen?

The many successes in educating people about the arts through television have occurred primarily in the performing arts. Take dance, for example. A dozen years ago, one or at most two dance programs were produced each year on public television. The dancers and choreographers themselves were afraid of close-ups; they were nervous about what might be exposed. The assumption was that the steps would be distorted by the cameras, reframed in another kind of space that was either too remote or too close, diminishing the step or making it larger than life. There were good grounds for such suspicions. Still, a few in public television persisted, arguing, flattering and planning, knowing that dance programs could be made to enhance the art in new ways and perhaps enlarge the audience.

Finally, the National Endowment for the Arts and the Corporation for Public Broadcasting and a few other contributors, mainly Exxon, decided to fund a two-year series of four dance programs to be called "Dance in America." The series is now celebrating its 10th anniversary. Along the way,

*Robert Kotlowitz is vice president for arts and humanities at WNET/Channel 13.*

George Balanchine, after working with his own great company for the series, began to rechoreograph some of his masterworks for presentations on the small screen. Before his death, he was planning works designed for television.

From the beginning of this series, the audience response was enormous, and it has grown from season to season. Many in that audience who had never seen a live dance performance became partisans of the companies they saw on television for the first time and joined the audience for others. Surely this response contributed to the sevenfold increase in the number of dance companies nationwide as well as to the financial health of those already in the field.

Taking chances often provided big payoffs. The first broadcast of *Giselle*, live from Lincoln Center, attracted and held for the entire evening more than 400,000 viewers in New York City alone. Surely there were not already that many *Giselle* fans; most viewers were simply curious to see what the ballet was all about, why it was still being danced after so many years. These viewers represented every demographic, racial, ethnic or neighborhood group in the city.

Curiosity is what usually attracts television audiences initially, creating unexpected successes for televised arts programming. The list is long and includes the complete Bach B-Minor Mass; staged performances of all the Monteverdi operas; 13 episodes of Evelyn Waugh's *Brideshead Revisited*; Martha Graham's greatest works; evenings with Paul Taylor, Merce Cunningham and Pilobolus; the entire Shakespeare canon; and the Ring Cycle from Bayreuth — this last attracting a weekly nationwide audience of two million.

Given this track record, the time has arrived for the visual arts to be presented more often on television. In fact, the time is overdue, given the visual nature of the medium and the development of video cassettes. Some splendid work has been accomplished. The Metropolitan Museum of Art has already produced distinguished educational programs on cassette, many of them linked directly to museum exhibits and activities and designed to make the Metropolitan's treasures known throughout the nation. WNET has produced individual programs, mostly documentaries, about the lives of artists, including Pablo Picasso and Georgia O'Keeffe. WNET collaborated with the Metropolitan on a program about the museum's American Wing. WNET's own production of "Women in Art" was as much sociological as aesthetic in content. All these programs have found substantial audiences on first screenings and in reruns.

WNET has now embarked on a $6-million venture called "Art of the Western World." This series is being prepared in collaboration with television networks in Austria and England and with advisers drawn from many major U.S. museums. It is being designed as an educational series and is scheduled for prime time, and thus must be entertaining and accessible to the unsophisticated viewer if stations in the system are to agree to carry it at all. Each hour broadcast can be easily broken down into two 28-minute segments for potential classroom use. It is expected that the series will ultimately be broadcast to a worldwide audience of a quarter of a billion people, at least some of whom will never have seen a painting or sculpture in any kind of setting. Special educational and viewer-guide materials, as well as a lavish trade book, will accompany the series.

By now series like this one are the mainstream of visual arts programming, although they are still only "first generation" in technique and modes of presentation. Indeed, most of the "Live from the Metropolitan Opera" broadcasts today differ little from the first one aired 35 years ago, except for the availability of stereophonic sound.

It is time now to move beyond conventional program concepts in the visual arts and to design new formats. Not everything on the screen has to be documentary in style, or explicatory or educational or even high-minded. Television is a natural show medium, permitting superb exposures of objects as well as people and events of importance.

One problem is that the scheduling of programs on the air is still in an elementary stage of development. At least on public television, there are different programs every 30, 60 or 90 minutes. These lengths, though commercially convenient, have become a cage for both broadcasters and viewers. Some subjects that need 15 minutes are inflated to 30; some that would work beautifully at 35 go on for 90 minutes or more. A new kind of broadcast schedule is needed, not to displace the old one but to add to its effectiveness. Four-minute programs, for example, each devoted to an individual artwork, could be broadcast at the beginning and the end of daily programming. They could also be used to fill out more conventional programs that for one reason or another fall short of the required length. Once enough four-minute modules have been accumulated, it takes only 15 to make a full hour of a program that could be intellectually coherent if planned properly. Such modules would help fulfill the old idea of a museum without walls to which everyone has easy access. Let a day open with an hour of arts programming and end with the same, in a leisurely and quiet tour of the great museums of the world.

Video cassettes also offer wide possibilities. With little incremental cost, two tracks of programming could be developed with supplementary material produced as part of a cassette rather than in a separate print medium. The Metropolitan Museum of Art and the National Gallery of Art developed videos that have already been aired on public television, and have thus been funded and paid for, so it would be possible to convert them fairly easily to cassettes for inexpensive sale.

More should be done to make the arts widely accessible through a medium with which people are already comfortable and which, with VCRs, they are using independent of previously determined scheduling. It has taken years for the idea of public television to seep into national consciousness; although its audience share has always been small compared with that of the networks, that share has been increasing by an average of 6 to 8 percent a year. More creative use of arts programming, through mini-modules or better use of cassettes, would arouse new curiosity and new interest and, in turn, would enhance access and greater pleasure for all.

**conclusion**

# ARTS, EDUCATION AND NONTRADITIONAL SETTINGS

## by Dale McConathy

Contributors to this seminar have concerned themselves largely with the personnel, the locations, the timing and the adult audiences for arts education within particular institutional contexts. Still remaining is the task for all to join in a definition of American culture, as it is and as it might become, so that efforts to transmit it to all members of the body politic can proceed with greater strength and focus. At least those of us working in arts education have started to discover the identities and activities of our colleagues in this venture; we are recognizing that we are not as alone as we had thought. Our thinking, our hopes and aspirations have perhaps gone much further as yet than our achievements.

## THE CULTURAL CONTEXT

At present, 55 percent of all education in this country occurs in nontraditional settings, partly as a result of the apparent disintegration of public education and the staggeringly high cost of traditional education at all levels. Whether in the classroom or "beyond" it, all may agree that the arts should be necessary components. But society is unclear about how to act on that agreement. A welcome consensus has stopped short of real, ongoing enactment of our dreams. Society is undecided about how this marriage of culture and education should be paid for. Further, there are no ways of evaluating the nontraditional programs that now exist. Thus all may agree that the arts are good for people, but no one is certain how that good takes place or whether, as a good, it should be built into the nation's political or economic agenda.

*Dale McConathy was chairperson of the Department of Art and Art Education at New York University.*

## Persisting Assumptions

One major implication evident in this seminar is that seemingly little of the society's highest culture has been transmitted other than through the middle-class delivery systems that have been purveying the arts all along. Even to raise such an issue may be something of a leap forward. Here, as well as elsewhere among arts professionals, there is a certain smugness about both the arts and education. Because arts professionals are involved with both, they feel they are on the side of the angels, believing, as they did a century ago, that exposing themselves to great ideas and great artworks makes them better people. They are great through their association with greatness, and as for those who do not join them, it is their loss.

Such views may be regarded either as justly self-congratulatory or as whistling in the dark. One's viewpoint may depend upon whether one is a member of the generation that saw the inception of the National Endowments, the states' arts councils, the missionary efforts of public broadcasting, the legislative mandates establishing education as a primary function of nonprofit institutions, the ascendancy of the corporate patron, the emphasis on fiscal soundness and business models for arts managers and the inclusion of popular programming in all the arts. Though such institutionalized successes are grounds for much satisfaction, they may also at the same time be adulterating an ability to assess the quality and the impact of the arts, contributing to a tendency to act on the basis of yearly spread sheets rather than on an ongoing consideration of the society and its needs—and the arts and their needs.

In any event, no matter how healthy or necessary these expanded patterns of patronage and programming have been, they remain based on assumptions about an ideal American society that is supposedly both hierarchical and characteristically white Anglo-Saxon Protestant, motivated by values articulated by a closed Eastern establishment and rooted in patriarchal ideas of social planning and public benefit that have changed little since the 1950s. The purveyors of such ideas of culture did not envision any real change in the distribution of the audiences for that culture, let alone in its content or form. Nonetheless, mass education, set off by the G.I. Bill, has undermined the validity of such earlier formulations and the traditional role of established educational and arts institutions.

For all of the positive consequences of mass education, including a reaction against the traditionally limited elitist views of culture and the assertion of their own traditions by proudly "unmeltable" ethnic groups, there has been the negative consequence of cutbacks in the teaching of Western civilization, of history, of values and ideas for their own sake. These movements are concurrent with the arts boom of the 1960s: the trends are surely related. Thus elite cultural institutions have responded to these pressures, asserting a greater cosmopolitanism and internationalism that links American corporations and diplomatic efforts in touring museum blockbusters and foreign performing-arts companies.

These more diversified programs may also be seen as a final assertion of social and cultural ideas stemming from the assumption that privileged elites were the primary sponsors and consumers of the arts. However, the upper-middle classes — college-educated, professional, affluent — have taken over as arts patrons. They now pay the majority of the arts bills, exerting a new influence on what is seen and heard. Their power at the box office and turnstile, as well as in the board room, administrative office and government agency, has begun to dictate programming and to reinforce existing leveling tendencies. They have brought the arts down (or up?) to their level — but not beyond. So although the size of arts audiences outstrips those for sporting events, the mega-audience for the arts has changed little in composition, attitudes and cultural horizons.

More problematic is the generational, and to some extent class-related, discontinuity in our society between those who have been directly socialized to the arts and those who have experienced such culture only through television. Today's average high-school senior has watched more than 20,000 hours of television, forming a basis for a particular understanding of culture unlike any that has occurred before. No matter the pluses or minuses of the mass media, their support for or negative influence on the arts, they are now a fact, with cumulative effects that cannot yet be estimated.

Perhaps because most senior professionals in arts organizations are of the "pre-TV" generation, this new presence in our midst is not fully comprehended. If development campaigns continue to be directed to the affluent rather than to the larger community, how can the audience be broadened — especially among those already and otherwise immersed in the media? Unless ways to do so are discovered, the arts as we know them may become extinct.

## Corporate Influence

Business has become more involved in arts in the last 25 years. Corporate executive officers have proclaimed themselves the new Medicis of culture in the United States. More than 800 corporate art collections have been formed. The arts have proved a highly effective way of raising popular acceptance of the way business is done, by convincing the public that support and public enjoyment of the arts is an important goal of corporate operations.

Although nineteenth-century businessmen often thought of their enterprises as utopian, only after the Second World War did U.S. corporations offer educational or training programs that not only taught company policy and prepared highly skilled specialists but also attempted to forge a special bond between the corporations and their employees. Though on-the-job training has been around forever, few companies have ventured into the larger arena to themselves develop and provide their own affiliate degree programs, to broaden the scope of in-house education and otherwise to try to enrich the lives of their rank-and-file employees outside the workplace, to extend their resources to the surrounding community or to teach as they might indeed be able.

So beyond noontime lectures, season tickets to theaters and museums and the display of contemporary art, most corporations have not considered the arts as a part of their educational programming. Generally, aside from the few enlightened examples mentioned during the seminar and certain enlightened areas such as Minneapolis-St. Paul, where some 200 corporations give wide support to the arts and actively involve all of their employees, the business sector can do much more. Even in mid-Manhattan, the vast majority of corporations do not pool their arts-support resources, do not share cooperative programs, apparently do not aim to act as neighbors. Rather, when cultural programming takes place at all, such educational efforts are largely self-enclosed, referring back to the corporate setting to reinforce its separateness, and therefore often duplicating the cultural efforts and investments of others. Clearly, without shared standards and with no clearinghouse to find out what else is going on, the contribution of corporations to nontraditional arts education is only vaguely understood and certainly has yet to realize its important potential.

## Federal Government Influence

In any event, the major educational force in the United States is no longer the schools and colleges, nor even the newly developing sphere of corporate-sponsored nontraditional education. Rather, it is the federal government.

Much government-sponsored education has been for the military and their families, especially those posted overseas, and otherwise for civil servants. But Uncle Sam is involved in many widespread arts and education programs, directly in the U.S. Information Agency, more indirectly through the Parks Service, which manages many small museums and historical sites, the General Services Administration, which can directly commission art works, and even the Department of Transportation, which has a "percent for art" provision in its funding guidelines.

There is, of course, the Smithsonian Institution, which, using the resources of its vast and varied collections, has long sought to address the generalist rather than the specialist in its public education programs. With an approach that has grown out of the new archaeology, the Smithsonian has tended to view its various holdings in terms of material culture, and to foster the study of social and economic systems rather than just to search for masterpieces. As a result, the Smithsonian has become a powerful force in recasting museum education, in particular, and a whole new view of cultural history, in general. Its efforts to improve museum access are consistent with these pedagogical aims.

Still, the play of government in cultural policy cannot help but shape the thinking and achievements of the institutions and the individuals who are given its financial support. The idea of government as arts educator and cultural transmitter is a decisive step away from earlier libertarian ideals. Efforts to cut back state support for the arts have been advanced by critics on both the right and the left, leaving the field confused for both proponents and antagonists. Here, too, as with the impact of the mass media and of corporate support, without agreed-upon criteria and rationales for particular kinds of arts education programs and their funding, it is difficult to evaluate fully the results of government cultural policies.

## LIFELONG LEARNING

If the status of the arts and education is low in the corporate setting and ambiguous in the context of government, the notion of lifelong learning has a similar status. Now our heterogeneous population is challenging the traditional division of life into three separate and distinct phases: education, work and retirement. As longevity increases, there is greater acceptance of the idea of second and third careers, an idea pioneered by the return of women to the work force. Today there are greater pressures on all to make career changes, acquire new skills and make better use of leisure time. Such new challenges and opportunities have brought many back to school. Such returnees often speak of their first education as preparation for a career and the return to school as preparation "to be themselves." Among such mature students, the arts often prove to be an integrative force and a mode of expression previously lacking.

However, for this population of students, the role of the arts is all too often defined as being therapeutic, with the students themselves defined as hobbyists, amateurs, too old for serious arts education and productive artmaking. Hidden in such definitions are assumptions about class, age and sex, about those whose artistic talent deserves nurturance versus those who are destined only to try to appreciate such talent in others. Yet with increasing longevity and greater education among all sectors of the population, the pressures to overcome such biases will increase.

Another received idea destructive to arts education for adults must be confronted. This is that the arts are a dessert course in our educational process: sweet and tasty but not necessarily nutritious. This idea not only places the arts in constant jeopardy regarding their status in the general curriculum, but also prevents them from being fully integrated into the learning process itself, whenever that takes place during the life span.

Further, the arts are part of a general packaging for cultural "consumption." People speak of "the art of wine," "the art of cosmetics," of "lifestyles" that can be adopted or changed as fashion dictates. People think there are shortcuts to culture. Art becomes a form of name-dropping; ballet is glittering acrobatics; chamber music is background sound while commuting. Thus society trivializes the arts, as it trivializes arts education and the motivations and capacities of the adults who would be the learners.

## THE NEW PURITANISM

If trivializing the arts is one threat to their survival, proponents of the New Puritanism have created another. They would censor them because of the power of the arts to undermine traditional morality and order. Added to the traditional American emphasis upon practical education and business and the increasing pressures to deal with severe social and political problems, this view sees arts philanthropy and arts education as too rich for the blood or too expensive for the public purse.

In response to such critiques, arts advocates point to recent studies demonstrating the economic impact of the arts. For example, the culture industries in New York annually account for about $1.5 billion in taxable income. Such big spending leads as well to the gentrification of previously derelict areas—leading in turn to criticism about a decrease in middle- and lower-income housing. Such emphases upon the wealth that the arts can engender have contributed as well toward a view of the artist as star or celebrity, identifying the arts with the commercial media. Yet though various studies show that parents now accept and even approve of arts careers for their children, their acceptance has not been paralleled by greatly increased enrollments in advanced art studies or professional schools.

Thus the anomalous position of the arts in the United States persists. Because few in the arts make a living at their art, and arts institutions depend heavily on subsidy, the arts professions — including those of arts education — have not gained full social acceptance. No wonder that arts educators do not, and probably will not for the foreseeable future, form a lobby with enough political clout to argue the case for the arts and arts education on their own merits. Efforts such as this seminar are a first step in disseminating information and pointing toward criteria that may help to unify the field. Such criteria must be enunciated clearly and bravely.

## COMMUNITIES OF MEMORY

The common assumption of participants in this seminar has been that, for the arts to exist and to have wide impact in a democracy, they must be available to everyone. Although we are on the verge of understanding that the arts are central to our ability to understand and assimilate experience of all kinds, acting upon this understanding is problematic. Still, however utopian are the vision and the goal, both are necessary.

To achieve them, we must recognize that the arts exist in three distinct but related forms, serving different social functions. First, the arts serve as both comfort and consolation, allowing people the expression and definition of emotions that may be more than they can bear alone. Second, the arts are also objects of contemplation and analysis. This is the view taken by most arts institutions, and it has largely been accepted as the basis for arts education. But finally, even more significantly, the arts foster sociability, a sense of community, contributing both to the profundity of religion and to entertainment as well.

In the recent sociological study *Habits of the Heart,* the authors propose that, with the decline of the nuclear family and vast changes in American institutions, the schools, churches, corporations and other social structures will take on much more of a therapeutic function. Museums, theaters, concert halls, zoos, botanical gardens and historic sites will acquire an increasingly important role as "communities of memory," transmitters of values and the shared experience of society. Colleagues in the workplace will assume new roles as quasi-family, teachers, mentors, friends. Through teaching and perpetuating the communities of common memory, as a society we can act with both freedom and joint purpose toward a better future.

The past two centuries have represented the greatest achievements in all the arts since the Greeks. What has truly revolutionized and strengthened the arts has been their sheer availability. The museum, the concert hall, the theater, the library—none has walls any longer, as Andre Malraux predicted. Technology and the mass media have taken the arts outside their traditional settings, and arts education far beyond the classroom.

The greater availability of the arts has changed their status. Their consumption is no longer confined to the few. Just as logical thinking spread across Western society at the end of the Middle Ages, the arts as a way of thinking are spreading today. To understand the extraordinary possibilities for the arts in nontraditional education, we must recognize a whole new group of people who may never actually make art, but who want to think, live and work artistically. These people—mature and already educated adults—have unprecedented expectations of themselves and the institutions that serve them. Their need for tools and materials and the training to use them, as well as the knowledge of their uses in the past, are all elements in the new nontraditional arts education.

Scientists and philosophers have begun to recognize the importance of metaphor in their thinking—the image that turns an abstraction into something real. Such transformative imagination is at play all the time and can be enriched in all of us. The music we hum, the images we retain, the phrases we repeat, our movements to fill empty time and space are all evidence of its constant activity. We are each at work on a symphony, a play, a painting all the time. We must all be allowed to use that freedom of transformative thinking to understand, to master, to simply accept or to better our complex world.

# appendix

# SELECTED BIBLIOGRAPHY

by David Pankratz

## Museum Education and Adults

Booth, Jeanette Hauck, Gerald H. Krockhauer and Paula R. Woods. *Creative Methods and Educational Techniques.* Springfield, Ill.: Charles C. Thomas Publishers, 1982.

Center for Museum Education. *Lifelong Learning/Adult Years — Sourcebook No. 1.* Washington, D.C.: George Washington University, 1978.

Chapman, Laura. "The Future and Museum Educators." *Museum News* 60 (July/August 1982):48-56.

Collins, Zipporah W., ed. *Museums, Adults and the Humanities: A Guide to Educational Programming.* Washington, D.C.: American Association of Museums, 1981.

Eisner, Elliot W. and Stephen M. Dobbs. *The Uncertain Profession: Observations on the State of Museum Education in Twenty American Art Museums.* Los Angeles: J. Paul Getty Center for Education in the Arts, 1986.

Goodman, Nelson. "The End of the Museum." *Journal of Aesthetic Education* 19, no. 2 (Summer 1985):53-62.

Horn, Adrienne. "The Adult Tour Dilemma." *Museum Education Anthology 1973-1983,* edited by Susan K. Nichols. Washington, D.C.: Museum Education Roundtable, 1984.

*Journal of Aesthetic Education,* Special Issue, "Art Museums and Education" 19, no. 2 (Summer 1985).

Levi, Albert William. "The Art Museum as an Agency of Culture." *Journal of Aesthetic Education* 19, no. 2 (Summer 1985):23-40.

Munley, Mary Ellen. *Catalysts for Change: The Kellogg Projects in Museum Education.* Washington, D.C.: The Kellogg Projects in Museum Education, 1986.

Newsom, Barbara Y. "A Decade of Uncertainty for Museum Educators." *Museum News* 58, no. 5 (May/June 1980):46-50.

Newsom, Barbara Y. and Adele Z. Silver, eds. *The Art Museum as Educator*. Berkeley: University of California Press, 1978.

Report of the Commission on Museums for a New Century. *Museums for a New Century*. Washington, D.C.: Association of American Museums, 1985.

Salazar, Susan Malins. *A Qualitative Investigation of Denver Art Museum Members in Relation to DAM Adult Programming*. Denver: Denver Art Museum, 1986.

Smith, Ralph A. "Art Museums and Education." *Journal of Aesthetic Education* 19, no. 2 (Summer 1985):5-12.

Williams, Patterson B. "Educational Excellence in Art Museums: An Agenda for Reform." *Journal of Aesthetic Education* 19, no. 2 (Summer 1985):105-23.

## Performing Arts and Adult Arts Education

Dawson, William M. *A Residency Handbook*. Madison, Wis.: Association of College, University and Community Arts Administrators, 1975.

Diamond, David, ed. *Outreach Programs and Community Services — 60-Second Survey #22*. New York: Theatre Communications Group, 1984.

Hart, Philip. *Orpheus in the New World: The Symphony Orchestra as an American Cultural Institution*. New York: W. W. Norton and Co., Inc., 1973.

Morison, Bradley G. and Julie Gordon Dalgleish. *Waiting in the Wings: A Larger Audience for the Arts and How to Develop It*. New York: American Council for the Arts, 1987.

OPERA America. "Adult Education: 1985 Survey Results and Program Examples" in *Working Ideas*. Washington, D.C.: OPERA America, 1985.

Sigman, Matthew. "Building New Audiences." *Symphony Magazine* 36, no. 4 (Aug./Sept. 1985):36-37.

Silverstein, Lynne, Bernard S. Rosenblatt and Robert F. Miller. *In, Through, and About — Education Workshops at an Arts Center*. St. Louis: CEMREL, Inc. and Education Program for the John F. Kennedy Center for the Performing Arts, 1982.

Truskot, Joseph, Anita Belofsky and Karen Kittilstad. *Orchestra Education Programs: A Handbook and Directory of Education and Outreach Programs*. Washington, D.C.: American Symphony Orchestra League, 1984.

## Arts Education and Older Adults

Balkema, John B. *The Creative Spirit: An Annotated Bibliography on the Arts, Humanities and Aging.* Washington, D.C.: The National Council on the Aging, Inc., 1986.

Cahill, Patti, ed. *The Arts, Humanities and Older Americans: A Catalogue of Program Profiles.* Washington, D.C.: The National Council on the Aging, Inc., 1981.

Gluck, Phyllis Gold. "Continuities and Diversities in Life-Long Education." *Lifelong Learning and the Visual Arts: A Book of Readings,* Donald H. Hoffman, Pearl Greenberg and Dale A. Fitzner, eds. Reston, Va.: National Art Education Association, 1980:67-71.

Greenberg, Pearl. *Visual Arts and Older People: Developing Quality Programs.* Springfield, Il.: Charles C. Thomas, Publisher, 1987.

Hoffman, Donald H., Pearl Greenberg and Dale H. Fitzner, eds. *Lifelong Learning and the Visual Arts: A Book of Readings.* Reston, Va.: National Art Education Association, 1980.

Hutchings, Ingrid and Susan McDonald. *The Perception and Use of Performing Arts Centers by the Elderly.* University of Illinois at Urbana-Champaign: Krannert Center for the Performing Arts, 1985.

Johnson, Alton C., et al. *Older Americans: The Unrealized Audience for the Arts.* Madison, Wis.: Center for Arts Administration, University of Wisconsin, 1975.

Jones, Jean Ellen. "Older Adults and Art: Research Needs." *Lifelong Learning and the Visual Arts: A Book of Readings,* Donald H. Hoffman, Pearl Greenberg and Dale A. Pitzner, eds. Reston, Va.: National Art Education Association, 1980:152-59.

Jones, Jean Ellen, guest editor. "Older Americans and the Arts." *Educational Gerontology* 8, no. 2 (1982).

Jones, Jean Ellen. *Teaching Art to Older Adults: Guidelines and Lessons.* Atlanta: Georgia State University, 1980.

Kaplan, Max, ed. *Leisure, Recreation, Culture and Aging: An Annotated Bibliography.* Washington, D.C.: The National Council on the Aging, Inc., 1982.

Kuhn, Marylou. "An Address: Toward a Philosophical Base for Life-Long Learning in the Arts." *Lifelong Learning and the Visual Arts: A Book of Readings,* Donald H. Hoffman, Pearl Greenberg and Dale A. Fitzner, eds. Reston, Va.: National Art Education Association, 1980:18-35.

McCutcheon, Priscilla. *Developing Older Audiences: Guidelines for Perform-*

*ing Arts Groups.* Washington, D.C.: The National Council on the Aging, Inc., 1985.

McCutcheon, Priscilla and Cathryn Wolf. *The Resource Guide to People, Places and Programs in Arts and Aging.* Washington, D.C.: The National Council on the Aging, Inc., 1985.

Moody, Harry R. *Aging and Cultural Policy.* Washington, D.C.: The National Council on the Aging, Inc., 1982.

Swaim, Richard C. "Educational and Cultural Programs for the Older Person: A Caveat." *Gerontology and Geriatrics Education* 3, no. 3 (1983):193-99.

Sunderland, Jacqueline T. *Older Americans and The Art.* Washington, D.C.: John F. Kennedy Center for the Performing Arts and The National Council on the Aging, Inc., 1972.

Sunderland, Jacqueline T., ed. *Arts and the Aging: An Agenda for Action.* Washington, D.C.: The National Council on the Aging, Inc., 1977.

Sunderland, Jacqueline T., ed. *Education: An Arts/Aging Answer.* Washington, D.C.: The National Council on the Aging, Inc., 1979.

The Cultural Education Collaborative. *Partners in Education: A Guide to Developing Cultural Programs for Adults.* Boston, CEC, 1981.

Weisberg, Nadia and Rosilyn Wilder, eds. *Creative Arts with Older Adults.* New York: Human Sciences Press, 1985.

White House Conference on the Aging. *Report of the Mini-Conference on the Arts, Humanities and Older Americans.* Washington, D.C.: The National Council on the Aging, Inc., 1981.

## Adult Arts Education in Nontraditional Settings

Brown, Katherine. "Turning a Poor Relative into a Rich Relative." *Art Education* 36, no. 1:36-37.

Business Committee for the Arts. "Corporations House Branch Museums: A New Development in Arts Support." *BCA News* (Jan./Feb. 1985):1, 8.

Business Committee for the Arts. "Businesses Nationwide Sponsor Performing Artists in the Workplace and the Community." *BCA News* (July/Aug. 1986):1.

Degge, Rogena M. "A Descriptive Study of Community Art Teachers with Implications for Teacher Preparation and Cultural Policy." *Studies in Art Education* 28, no. 3 (Spring 1987):164-75.

Eurich, Nell D. *Corporate Classrooms: The Learning Business.* Princeton, N.J.: The Carnegie Foundation for the Advancement of Teaching, 1985.

Hannun, Becky, ed. *Art in the Marketplace*. Columbia, Md.: The Rouse Company, 1984.

Howarth, Shirley Reiff, ed. *Directory of Corporate Art Collections*. Largo, Fla.: International Art Alliance, 1984.

Kaplan, Max. "The Arts and Recreation." In Max Kaplan, *Leisure: Perspectives on Education and Policy*. Washington, D.C.: National Education Association, 1978.

Keens, William, interviewer, "Serving Up Culture: The Whitney and Its Branch Museums." *Museum News* 64, no. 4 (April 1986):22-28.

Kuhn, Marylou,. ed. "Symposium: The Locales of Adult Art Education." *Art Education* 18, no. 9 (1965).

Kuhn, Marylou. "Where the Action Is: Upsurge in Arts in the Community." *Studies in Art Education* 16, no. 2 (1975):3-4.

Kuhn, M. and J. Hutchens. "Facilitating Educational Access to Social Networks for the Arts." *Art Education* 39, no. 4 (July 1986):37-41.

Lane, Barry. "Bringing Artists and Audiences Closer — Affiliate Artists." *New York Times,* Sunday, November 6, 1983.

Landrum, Baylor. *Labor-Management Support for the Arts Demonstration Projects, Phase One — Final Report*. Louisville, Ky.: Greater Louisville Fund for the Arts, April 1986.

Mangum, Barry D. "Challenges and Possibilities in Arts Programming." *Parks and Recreation* 14, no. 7 (July 1979):24-27.

Mangum, Barry D. "A Giant Step Forward for the Arts in Leisure." *Parks and Recreation* 17, no. 7 (July 1982):30-31.

National Jewish Welfare Board. "Cultural Arts and Education." *Zarkor* 4, no. 3 (Feb. 1983):1-9.

Rosen, Randy. "Education: The New Frontier in Corporate Art." *Corporate Art Report* 2, no. 1 (March/April 1984):2.

Shiff, Bennett. *Arts in Park and Recreation Settings*. Washington, D.C.: National Endowment for the Arts, National Park Service and National Park and Recreation Association, 1973.

Smith, Ralph A. "Cultural Services, Aesthetic Welfare, and Educational Research." *Studies in Art Education* 16, no. 2 (1975):5-11.

Sowder, Lynn. "Education as Part of the Corporate Art Program." *Corporate Art Report* 1, no. 3 (July/Aug. 1983):4.

Useem, Michael. "New Opportunities for Management Development and Executive Education." In *Educating Managers: Executive Effectiveness*

*Through Liberal Learning,* edited by Joseph S. Johnston, Jr. San Francisco: Jossey-Bass Publishers, 1986.

YMCA-USA. *Arts Program Survey Findings.* Rosemont, Ill.: YMCA-USA, 1987.

## Broadcast Media and the Arts

Beck, Kirsten. *Cultivating the Wasteland: Can Cable Put the Vision Back in TV?* New York: American Council for the Arts, 1983.

Carey, John. *Telecommunications Technologies and Public Broadcasting.* Washington, D.C.: Corporate for Public Broadcasting, 1986.

Hillard, Robert C. *Television and Adult Education.* Cambridge, Mass.: Schenkman Books, Inc., 1985.

Lipman, Samuel. "Broadcast Music." In S. Lipman, *The House of Music: Art in an Era of Institutions.* Boston: David R. Godine Publishers, 1984:274-88.

Mahoney, Sheila, Nick DeMartino and Robert Stengel. *Keeping PACE With the New Television: Public Television and Changing Technology.* The Carnegie Corporation of New York. New York: UNU Books International, 1980.

Riccobono, John A. *Out-of-School Learning Among Children, Adolescents, and Adults: Report of the Findings From the Home Information Technology Study.* Washington, D.C.: Corporation for Public Broadcasting and Center for Statistics, July 1986.

Robinson, John P. *Cultural Participation in the Arts: Final Report on the 1985 Survey.* Vol I prepared for the Research Division, National Endowment for the Arts. Washington, D.C.: National Endowment for the Arts, 1986.

## Adult and Continuing Education

Brookfield, Stephen D. *Understanding and Facilitating Adult Learning.* San Francisco: Jossey-Bass Publishers, 1986.

Carr, David. "Mediation as a Helping Presence in Cultural Institutions." In *Involving Adults in the Educational Process,* edited by S. H. Rosenblum, *New Directions for Continuing Education,* no. 26. San Francisco: Jossey-Bass Publishers (June 1985):87-96.

Carr, David. "Self-Directed Learning in Cultural Institutions." In *Self-Directed Learning: From Theory to Practice,* edited by Stephen Brookfield, *New Directions for Continuing Education,* no. 25. San Francisco: Jossey-Bass Publishers (March 1985):51-62.

Cross, Patricia K. *Adults as Learners*. San Francisco: Jossey-Bass Publishers, 1981.

Dacus, Donna L. and Philip M. Nowlen, eds. *Conference Proceedings, The Future of the Arts and Humanities: How, Where and With Whom.* Washington, D.C.: Division of Humanities, Arts, and Sciences, National University Continuing Education Association, 1986.

Donaldson, Joe F. "An Integrated Program of Noncredit Lecture/Discussion Series in the Arts—University of Illinois at Urbana-Champaign." In *Innovations in Continuing Education: 1981 Award-Winning New Programs.* Washington, D.C.: National University Continuing Education Association and the American College Testing Program, 1981.

Friere, Paulo. *The Politics of Education: Culture, Power, and Liberation.* South Hadley, Mass.: Bergin and Garvey Publishers, Inc., 1985.

Hiemstra, Roger. *Lifelong Learning.* Lincoln, Neb.: Professional Educators' Publications, 1976.

Hoyle, Cyril O. *Patterns of Learning: New Perspectives on Life-Span Education.* San Francisco: Jossey-Bass Publishers, 1984.

Knowles, Malcolm S. *The Adult Learner: A Neglected Species,* 3rd ed. Houston: Gulf Publishing Co., 1984.

Knox, Alan B. and Roscoe L. Shields. "Emerging Directions in Adult Art Education." *Art Education* 18, no. 19 (1965): 25-32.

Kuhn, Marylou, guest editor. "Continuing Art Education for Adults." *Art Education* 8, no. 9 (Dec. 1965).

Tough, A. M. *The Adult's Learning Projects,* 2nd ed. Toronto: The Ontario Institute for Studies in Education, 1979.

## Cultural Policy, Funding and Adult Arts Education

Balfe, Judith and Margaret Jane Wyszomirski, eds. *Art, Ideology, and Politics.* New York: Praeger Publishers, 1985.

Barzun, Jacques. "A Surfeit of Art and Why Government Need Not Encourage It." *Harper's* 273, no. 1634 (July 1986):45-49.

Berman, Ronald. *Culture and Politics.* Lanham, Md.: University Press of America, 1984.

Cwi, David and Albert Diehl. *In Search of a Regional Policy for the Arts—Phase 1.* Baltimore: Johns Hopkins University, 1975.

DiMaggio, Paul J. "The Nonprofit Instrument and the Influence of the Marketplace on Policies in the Arts." In *The Arts and Public Policy in the*

*United States,* edited by W. McNeil Lowry. Englewood Cliffs, N.J.: Prentice-Hall, Inc., 1984.

DiMaggio, Paul J. *The Role of Independent Foundations in Support of the Arts.* Report to the Ford Foundation, September 11, 1985.

Gans, Herbert J. *Popular Culture and High Culture: An Analysis and Evaluation of Taste.* New York: Basic Books, Inc., Publishers, 1974.

Hoggart, Richard. *An English Temper.* New York: Oxford University Press, 1982.

Kelley, Owen. *Community, Art and the State: Storming the Citadels.* London: Comedia Publishing, 1984.

Lipman, Samuel. "Art, Patronage, and Education." *Design for Arts in Education* 87, no. 6 (July/Aug. 1986):32-38.

Mulcahy, Kevin V. and C. Richard Swain, eds. *Public Policy and the Arts.* Boulder, Colo.: Westview Press, 1982.

National Endowment for the Arts. *Five-Year Plan, 1986-1990.* Washington, D.C.: National Endowment for the Arts, 1983.

## ABOUT THE AMERICAN COUNCIL FOR THE ARTS

The American Council for the Arts (ACA) is one of the nation's primary sources of legislative news affecting all of the arts and serves as a leading advisor to arts administrators, educators, elected officials, arts patrons and the general public. To accomplish its goal of strong advocacy of the arts, ACA apromotes public debate in various national, state and local forums; communicates as a publisher of books, joiurnals, Vantage Point magazine and ACA UpDate; provides information services through its extensive arts education, policy and management library; and has as its key policy issues arts education, the needs of individual artists, private-sector initiataives, and international cultural relations.

MAJOR CONTRIBUTORS
GOLDEN BENEFACTORS
($75,000 and up)
American Telephone & Telegraph
Company
Gannett Foundation
Southwestern Bell
BENEFACTORS ($50,000-$74,999)
Aetna Life & Casualty Company
The Ahmanson Foundation
National Endowment for the Arts
SUSTAINERS ($25,000-$49,999)
American Re-Insurance Co.
Mr. and Mrs. Jack S. Blanton, Sr.
The Coca-Cola Company
Eleanor Naylor Dana Trust
Interlochen Arts Center
Johnson & Johnson
Philip Morris Companies, Inc.
New Jersey State Council on the
Arts
The Reed Foundation
Sears, Roebuck & Co.
Elton B. Stephens
Mr. and Mrs. Richard L. Swig
SPONSORS ($15,000-$24,999)
Bozell, Jacobs, Kenyon & Eckhardt
Geraldine R. Dodge Foundation
Exxon Corporation
IBM Corporation
The Ruth Lilly Foundation
Mutual Benefit Life
Peat Marwick & Main
Reverend and Mrs. Alfred R.
Shands III
Rockefeller Foundation
The San Francisco Foundation
Mr. John Straus
PATRONS ($10,000-$14,999)
Ashland Oil, Inc.
Equitable Life Assurance Society
Toni K. Goodale
The Irvine Company
Susan R. Kelly
N.W. Ayer, Inc.
Mrs. Charles Peebler
Murray Charles Pfister
New York Community Trust
The Prudential Foundation

Mr. and Mrs. Paul Schorr III
Starr Foundation
DONORS ($5,000-$9,999)
The Allstate Foundation
American Stock Exchange, Inc.
Ameritech
The Arts, Education and
Americans, Inc.
Batus, Inc.
Bell Atlantic
Mary Duke Biddle Foundation
Boeing Company
Chase Manhatten Bank
CIGNA Corporation
Dayton Hudson Foundation
Joseph Drown Foundation
Jeaneane B. Duncan
Mr. and Mrs. Frederick Dupree, Jr.
Federated Investors, Inc.
The First Boston Corporation
Ford Motor Company Fund
Gannett Outdoor
Goldman, Sachs & Company
Mr. and Mrs. John Hall
David H. Harris
Louis Harris
The Hartford Courant
Howard S. Kelberg
Ellen Liman
The Joe and Emily Lowe
Foundation, Inc.
Lewis Manilow
MBIA, Inc.
Merrill Lynch, Pierce, Fenner &
Smith Inc.
Mobil Foundation, Inc.
Morgan Guaranty Trust Company
J.P. Morgan Securities
Morgan Stanley & Co.
Morrison-Knudsen Corporation
New York Times Company
Foundation
Pacific Telesis Group
RJR Nabisco
General Dillman A. Rash
Mr. David Rockefeller, Jr.
Henry C. Rogers
Mr. and Mrs. LeRoy Rubin
Shell Companies Foundation
Allen M. Turner

Warner Lambert Company
Whirlpool Foundation
Xerox Corporation
**CONTRIBUTORS ($2,000-$4,999)**
Abbott Laboratories
Alcoa Foundation
Allied Corporation
American Electric Power Company, Inc.
American Express Foundation
Mr. and Mrs. Curtis L. Blake
Gerald D. Blatherwick
Edward Block
Borg-Warner Co.
Mrs. Eveline Boulafendis
Donald L. Bren
Bristol-Myers Fund
Mr. and Mrs. Martin Brown
C.W. Shaver
Terri and Timothy Childs
Chevron USA, Inc.
Robert Cochran
Mr. and Mrs. Hill Colbert
Mr. and Mrs. Donald G. Conrad
Barbaralee Diamonstein-Spielvogel
Mr. and Mrs. Charles W. Duncan, Jr.
Mrs. George Dunklin
Eastman Kodak Company
Emerson Electric Co.
Ethyl Corporation
GFI/KNOLL International Foundation
Donald R. Greene
Eldridge C. Hanes
Mr. and Mrs. Irving B. Harris
Ruth and Skitch Henderson
Henry C. Kates
John Kilpatrick
Knight Foundation
Kraft, Inc.
Mr. Robert Krissel
Marsh & McLennan Companies
Mr. and Mrs. John B. McCory
The Monsanto Fund
Robert M. Montgomery, Jr.
Velma V. Morrison
New York Life Foundation
Overbrook Foundation
Mr. and Mrs. Thomas Pariseleti

Procter & Gamble Fund
Raytheon Company
Mr. and Mrs. Richard S. Reynolds III
Judith and Ronald S. Rosen
Rubbermaid, Inc.
Sara Lee Corporation
Frank Saunders
David E. Skinner
Union Pacific Foundation
Mrs. Gerald H. Westby
Westinghouse Electric Fund
Mrs. Thomas Williams, Jr.
**FRIENDS ($1,000-$1,999)**
Morris J. Alhadeff
Mr. and Mrs. Arthur G. Altschul
AmSouth Bank N.A.
Archer Daniels Midland Co.
Mr. Wallace Barnes
Bell South
Mr. and Mrs. Evan Beros
Biney & Smith
T. Winfield Blackwell
Houston Blount
Bowne of Atlanta, Inc.
William A. Brady, M.D.
Alan Cameros
Mr. and Mrs. George Carey
Chris Carson
Mrs. George P. Caulkins
Mr. Campbell Cawood
Mrs. Jay Cherniack
Chesebrough-Pond's Inc.
Chrysler Corporation Fund
Citizens and Southern Corporation
David L. Coffin
Mr. and Mrs. Marshall Cogan
Thomas B. Coleman
Cooper Industries
Mrs. Howard Cowan
Cowles Charitable Trust
John G. Crosby
Mrs. Crittenden Currie
David L. Davies
Eugene C. Dorsey
Ronald and Hope Eastman
EBSCO Industries, Inc.
Mrs. Hubert Everist
Mary and Kent Frates
Stephanie French